£4

QUEEN VICTORIA

Her Life and Legacy

QUEEN VICTORIA

Her Life and Legacy

Paul Kendall

FRONTLINE
BOOKS

Queen Victoria: Her Life and Legacy

This edition published in 2022 by Frontline Books,
An imprint of Pen & Sword Books Ltd,
Yorkshire - Philadelphia

ISBN 978 1 39901 831 9

CIP data records for this title are available from the British Library

Pen & Sword Books Limited incorporates the imprints of Atlas, Archaeology, Aviation, Discovery, Family History, Fiction, History, Maritime, Military, Military Classics, Politics, Select, Transport, True Crime, Air World, Frontline Publishing, Leo Cooper, Remember When, Seaforth Publishing, The Praetorian Press, Wharncliffe Local History, Wharncliffe Transport, Wharncliffe True Crime and White Owl.

PEN & SWORD BOOKS LTD
47 Church Street, Barnsley, South Yorkshire, S70 2AS, England
E-mail: enquiries@pen-and-sword.co.uk
Website: www.pen-and-sword.co.uk

Or
PEN AND SWORD BOOKS
1950 Lawrence Rd, Havertown, PA 19083, USA
E-mail: Uspen-and-sword@casematepublishers.com

For more information on our books, please visit
www.frontline-books.com, email info@frontline-books.com
or write to us at the above address.

Printed and bound by CPI Group (UK) Ltd, Croydon, CR0 4YY

Typeset in 10/14pt Adobe Caslon by SJmagic DESIGN SERVICES, India.

Contents

Introduction

This book is about the life and legacy of one of the most iconic sovereigns in British history. Queen Victoria was the fifth in line to succeed the British throne when she was born in 1837 and was an unlikely heir. The possibility of her becoming sovereign of the British Isles was extremely remote because her father was not the first child of George III, but his fourth issue. Eight months after her birth, Victoria's father died on 23 January 1820 of pneumonia and her grandfather, King George III, passed away six days later. The Prince Regent succeeded him to become King George IV. His daughter, Princess Charlotte, died shortly after giving birth to a stillborn child in 1817. Her death was followed by the next in line, the death of Prince Frederick, the Duke of York in 1827. When George IV died on 26 June 1830, his surviving brother, William IV, ascended the throne. The Duke of Kent's brothers did not have any surviving legitimate children, which meant that after the death of William IV, Victoria became heir presumptive to the throne and one of Britain's most notable and iconic monarchs.

For nearly a century, Victoria held the record for serving as the longest reigning British monarch, until her reign lasting sixty-three years and seven months was surpassed on 9 September 2015 by the reign of her great-great-granddaughter, Elizabeth II. When Victoria ascended the throne on 20 June 1837, she became the sixth successive monarch from the House of Hanover, which was of German origin. At that time, royalty was not respected by the populace and people no longer looked up to their sovereign with reverence. On her ascension in 1837 the nation had gained in Victoria a sovereign who would be respected with adoration and reverence, such esteem that no ruler had experienced for centuries.

Given that Britain was a patriarchal society when Victoria ascended the throne and that there had not been a female sovereign since Queen Anne in 1724; questions were asked whether the princess, aged eighteen, would be capable of reigning as monarch. Unlike her predecessor, Elizabeth I, who proclaimed that she had the 'body of a weak and feeble woman, but the heart and stomach of a king', Victoria did not try to rule as a king, but to govern as a woman, while being a wife and mother. She was a slender woman, 5ft 2in in height; and would prove that she was highly competent to serve as sovereign, despite it being a male-dominated world.

At the very start of her reign, she took an interest in politics, played an active part in the machinations of government and worked with ten Prime Ministers. Victoria was a formidable sovereign who could assert herself and stand her ground.

Britain was not a democracy at the beginning of Victoria's reign; it was governed by the aristocracy and people who owned land and property. Members of Parliament had to own land to make them eligible for election and they did not represent the entire nation. Three months after Victoria's birth, on 16 August 1819, British cavalry charged into a crowd of between 60,000 and 80,000 factory workers, with their wives and children, who were peacefully protesting for reformation of the parliamentary representation in St Peter's Field, Manchester, killing and wounding an undetermined number of the demonstrators. This act in which the British Army attacked the people whom they were meant to protect was known as the Peterloo Massacre and it would create division between the working and ruling classes.

The challenge to the existing elitist political system was among the reform issues that her Government confronted throughout her sovereignty.

Victoria broke down barriers between sovereign and her subjects, especially her soldiers, paying regular visits to hospitals in England to visit the wounded to provide words of comfort and to assess the state of hospitals and ensure that the standards of health care for the British Army and for the nation were improved. Victoria was also responsible for the creation of the campaign medals and the prestigious Victoria Cross, becoming the first sovereign to insist on presenting those decorations in person. Victoria was responsible for establishing the tradition of the white wedding, wearing a white bridal dress to ensure that her subjects could see her. She made efforts to make her more accessible to the people she ruled. Appearances on the balcony at Buckingham Palace during occasions of national celebration was a custom that she began and this tradition continues today.

By 1897, she would become the most powerful woman in the world, being in control of the British Empire, which spanned nearly a quarter of the surface of the globe, and during that year the sixtieth year of her reign was celebrated in Britain and across the Empire.

Paul Kendall
Folkestone, 2021

Acknowledgements

This book would not have been possible without the assistance of the following individuals. I am extremely grateful to Margaret Mackay for allowing me access to Victoria's royal arms, which are displayed at the Highgate Literary and Science Institute, South Grove, Highgate. I thank the Dean and Chapter of Westminster for use of image of the Coronation Chair. I extend my gratitude to the Anne S.K. Brown Military Collection, Brown University Library, for allowing use of images from its collection. I thank Sergeant Paul Herron for kindly taking images of the Officer's Mess at Royal School of Military Engineering in Chatham. I thank Tim Spriddell for the image of the statue of Dickens. I am indebted to Coralie Clover at The Princess of Wales Royal Regiment Museum, Dover Castle, for kindly providing me with images of Victoria's scarf. I am grateful to Royal Archives and Her Majesty Queen Elizabeth II for allowing me to quote from Victoria's journals. I thank Robert Mitchell for his invaluable assistance with many of the images. Finally, I thank my partner, Tricia Newsome, for her continued support in all my projects.

1

Kensington Palace

Birthplace of Queen Victoria

Kensington Palace had been used as a royal residence since 1689, after the throne of King James II was usurped during the bloodless coup known as the 'Glorious Revolution' by King William III. Together with his wife Mary, William III sought a new country home and decided upon acquiring Nottingham House, situated close to Kensington, which was at that time a rural village in the suburbs of London. They commissioned Sir Christopher Wren to transform Nottingham House into the royal palace that would be known as Kensington Palace and would later become Victoria's birthplace.

It was in a first-floor apartment in Kensington Palace that Victoria Mary Louise, Duchess of Kent, daughter of Francis, Duke of Saxe-Coburg-Saalfeld, gave birth to Princess Victoria at 4.15 am on 24 May 1819, in the presence of her father, Edward, Duke of Kent. The room in which she was born was originally a dining room, but when the duchess arrived it was considered suitable as a place for the baby to be born because the kitchens were situated directly below on the ground floor and were able to supply hot water. There was also an adjoining room where dignitaries such as the Archbishop of Canterbury, the Lord Chancellor the Marquis of Lansdown and several ministers could witness the birth. Two doctors delivered the baby, including Charlotte Heidenreich von Siebold, Germany's first female gynaecologist, who had accompanied the duchess from Germany. After Victoria was delivered safely, the Duke of Kent wrote, 'it is not possible to show more activity, more zeal and more knowledge than [Siebold has done].'[1] Three months later on 26 August 1819, Siebold delivered Victoria's cousin and future husband, Prince Albert, at Schloss Rosenau, near Coburg, Germany. On the day of her birth, Victoria was fifth in line to the throne after King George III's four eldest sons.

Exactly a month after her birth, Princess Victoria was christened by Charles Manners-Sutton, the Archbishop of Canterbury, in the Cupola Room in Kensington Palace at 3 pm on 24 June 1819. The Royal Gold Font was temporarily removed from the Tower of London and crimson velvet coverings from the Chapel Royal, St James's Palace, were brought to Kensington Palace for the occasion. Her uncle, George, the Prince Regent, was present at the ceremony

---

1. Williams, Kate, *Becoming Queen* (Arrow, London, 2009), p.140.

Victoria was born in a room on the first floor. If you count from the left on that floor, the tenth to twelfth windows belong to the room in which Victoria was born. During later years, Victoria's daughter, Princess Louise, sixth of her nine children, sculptured the marble statue that stands at the entrance to Kensington Palace. It depicts a young Victoria wearing coronation robes. It was unveiled by the Queen on 28 June 1893. (Author's Collection)

and Emperor Alexander of Russia was represented by the Duke of York. The Prince Regent loathed his younger brother, Edward, and was indignant that he had produced an heir to the throne that would eventually succeed him. He did not want this event to be perceived as the christening of a potential future monarch and dispensed with pomp and ceremony on this occasion. The Duke of Kent wanted to name his daughter Elizabeth, but the Prince Regent also dictated the name of the newly born princess, who was christened Alexandrina Victoria.

Smallpox was an infectious disease that was prevalent during the nineteenth century. In August 1819, at Kensington Palace, Princess Victoria became the first royal baby to be inoculated using Edward Jenner's vaccination.

When Princess Victoria was aged three, she nearly died in an accident when she was thrown from a pony carriage, which was driven by her mother in the gardens of Kensington Palace. Private John Maloney went to her aid by clutching the infant's dress before she was crushed by the carriage.

2

Royal Glen Hotel, Sidmouth

Edward, Duke of Kent, father of Princess Victoria died here.

There is a plaque in Room 15 in the hotel, with the inscription 'The room was occupied by her most Gracious Majesty Queen Victoria 1819-1820'. During her brief stay, the future queen nearly lost her life when a bullet fired by a boy shooting birds nearly hit her in this room. It was here where her father died on 23 January 1820.

The building was initially named King's Cottage after its owner, a Mr King, who transformed it into a Gothic villa with Regency interiors. The name was later changed to Woolbrook Cottage or Woolbrook Glen in 1817, when it was purchased by Major-General Edward Baynes. During December 1819, Edward, Duke of Kent, rented the cottage to spend time with his wife and his daughter Victoria, who was only seven months old.

Immediately after Queen Victoria arrived at the cottage at Sidmouth, a boy who was shooting birds was conducting this pursuit close to the cottage, so close that a shot from his

A view of the Royal Glen Hotel, Sidmouth. (Author's Collection)

Princess Victoria stayed in this room in 1820 and it was here that the bullet fired by the small boy came through the window and nearly killed her while she was in the arms of her nurse. (Author's Collection)

This plaque in Room 15 at the Royal Glen Hotel commemorates Victoria's stay. (Author's Collection)

gun broke the window of the nursery and nearly killed the baby Princess Victoria.[2] The Duke of Kent wrote on 30 December 1819:

> The dangerous practice of inexperienced persons being trusted with guns had yesterday been nearly attended with disastrous consequences: an apprentice boy, shooting at small birds, had the hardihood to approach so near the residences of their Royal Highnesses, that the shot broke the windows of the nursery, and passed very near the head of the infant Princess, who was in the arms of the nurse.[3]

The window is now marked by a coloured pane of glass. If the baby Victoria had died in this accident, British history would have taken a different direction.

2. *Hampstead and Highgate Express*, 18 June 1887.

3. Gurney, op. cit., p.54.

3

Albion House, Ramsgate

Princess Victoria frequently visited Ramsgate with her mother and during the 1820s lived at Townley House. In 1835, they stayed at Albion House, which overlooks the harbour.

In order to raise the public profile of Princess Victoria as future heir to the throne and prepare her for that role, the Duchess of Kent and Sir John Conroy arranged annual Royal Progresses, which were tours across England and Wales. William IV was not happy about these unsanctioned tours across the country because the public could perceive Princess Victoria as a rival instead of an heir. Ramsgate, in Kent, was a favourite retreat for the Duchess of Kent and her daughter. Their first visit took place on 23 August 1823, when the Duchess of Kent, accompanied by her brother Leopold, arrived with Princess Victoria by steamer from London.

Victoria stayed at Albion House, Ramsgate, from 29 September 1835 to 12 January 1836. The young princess observed from the hotel window the steamer carrying her uncle Leopold, who since 1831 had been King of Belgium, enter the harbour on the first day of her visit. The royal party attracted unwarranted attention and intrusions. It was reported that the:

> rude curiosity of the vulgar during this time led them to climb the railings in front of Albion House, so as to overlook the lower suite of rooms where the royal party generally assembled. Some inhabitants of Ramsgate, without consulting the Duchess of Kent, hired constables at their own expense, and placed them about the house to prevent the continuance of these impertinencies. The illustrious party no sooner became aware of what was done than Sir John Conroy was commissioned to send these constables away, and to tell them that neither the duchess nor the princess required any such guard. The mob thus left to themselves their idle curiosity soon exhausted itself.[4]

On 7 October Leopold left Ramsgate to return home to Belgium. Victoria began to feel ill during that same day. She had caught typhoid and was dangerously ill. Suffering from a high fever and fatigue, she was confined to her bed for three weeks. Incapacitated and weak as she convalesced, Conroy saw this as an opportunity to force Victoria to sign a letter confirming his appointment as her private secretary in the event she became queen. Victoria found the

---

4. *Bell's Messenger*, 26 June 1836.

Albion House, Ramsgate, where Princess Victoria stayed in 1835 and 1836. She resided in a room on the first floor, above where the blue plaque is positioned. (Author's Collection)

strength and courage to refuse this contrived attempt by Conroy to advance and consolidate his own position within the royal court. This act would cause tension between Victoria and her mother. It would also impact upon him personally when Victoria would reject him as a personal aid when she eventually became queen. Victoria rallied and regained her health. She was able to enjoy her stay at Ramsgate and her journal mentioned her visits to the pier looking at the foreign vessels that berthed in the harbour.

4

Statue of King William IV

Death of William IV.

This statue of William IV was unveiled in December 1844 at the junction of King William Street and Cannon Street. This was the first granite statue erected in London and faced southwards towards London Bridge, which William had opened in 1831. Increasing traffic volumes entering the City of London and the construction of an underground pedestrian subway that could not support the statue prompted its transfer to Greenwich Park in 1935, where it still stands. The statue took three years to produce due to the difficulties of carving hard granite. It is 15ft high and he is dressed in the uniform of a Lord High Admiral, wearing the order of the garter. William IV served in the Royal Navy and was known as the sailor king.

William IV became the oldest monarch to ascend the British throne when he succeeded his brother in 1830, aged sixty-four, and would reign for seven years. He fathered ten illegitimate children with his mistress, the actress Dorothea Jordan, with whom he cohabited for twenty years. He eventually married Princess Adelaide of Saxe-Meiningen, but despite conceiving five children, none of them survived. In 1830, William IV considered the prospect of not having an heir, so at his instigation, Parliament passed the Regency Act. This designated the Duchess of Kent as Regent in the event that he died before Victoria's eighteenth birthday. However, the king became frustrated that he could not spend time with his niece, of whom he was very fond. William IV, being the 'sailor king', declared that, 'It will touch every sailor's heart to have a girl Queen to fight for. They'll be tattooing her face on their arms and I'll be bound they'll all think she was christened after Nelson's ship.'[5]

William IV resented deeply that Victoria was kept deliberately from Court, and he objected to the Duchess of Kent touring the country with Victoria emulating a royal progress. When they visited Welshpool on 2 August 1832, they were received with a royal gun salute and he ordered that this practice be discontinued. During 1835 the Duchess of Kent sought permission to conduct refurbishments and make use of other rooms at Kensington Palace, but

---

5. Ponsonby, Arthur, *Queen Victoria* (Camelot Press Ltd, London, 1933), p.13.

The statue of King William IV that is located in the north-western corner of Greenwich Park. (Author's Collection)

the king refused. When he inspected the palace on 20 August 1836, he found that the Duchess of Kent had occupied seventeen rooms that he had reserved for himself and he was furious that she had ordered refurbishment and extension to her apartment without his consent. The king did not have confidence in her ability to act as regent and publicly declared in her presence at a banquet in St George's Hall, Windsor Castle, to celebrate his seventy-first and his final birthday on 21 August 1836, that he was determined to live until Victoria reached eighteen years old in order to avoid a regency, where her mother, who was influenced by inappropriate advisers such as Conroy, would rule the country.

Although, at that moment, Victoria was seventeen years old, William was confident in her ability to rule Britain as queen. William IV fulfilled his wish to live until Victoria had reached the age when she could succeed him. He died of bronchopneumonia and cardiac failure at Windsor Castle during the early hours on 20 June 1837 within a month of Victoria's eighteenth birthday and there was no need for a regency.

5

Painting Depicting Victoria Receiving the News of her Accession to the Throne

Princess Victoria Succeeded King William IV as Queen of Britain and Ireland on 20 June 1837.

Victoria was made aware that William IV was close to death. When her uncle passed away on 20 June 1837, she immediately became his successor as sovereign. Lord Francis Conyngham, the Lord Chamberlain and William Howley, the Archbishop of Canterbury, who were attending the ailing king during his last hours, immediately dashed from Windsor Castle to Kensington Palace to notify Victoria of the news and that she was now Queen of Great Britain and Ireland. The journey by horse took three hours, arriving at the palace at 5 am, where they experienced difficulty on entering. It would take a further hour for them to gain access to the princess. The gatekeeper was asleep and once aroused they entered the courtyard. They eventually entered the palace, where they were ushered into a room and left unattended. After some time, they rang a bell to get some attention. A tired servant had been woken from bed and they requested an immediate audience with the princess relating to business of extreme urgency. Howley and Conyngham were again left to their own devices until they rang the bell a second time. The princess's attendant responded and advised them that Her Royal Highness was asleep and had strict instructions that she was not to be disturbed. Howley and Conyngham responded that, 'We are come on business of State to the Queen, and even her sleep must give way to that.'[6] The servant realised the seriousness of the situation and went to the princess's bedchamber. According to Francis Williams-Wynn, who kept a diary at the time, 'In a few minutes she (the Queen) came into the room in a loose white nightgown and shawl, her nightcap thrown off, and her hair falling on her shoulders, her feet in slippers, tears in her eyes, but perfectly collected and dignified.'[7] It was from that moment for the remainder of her life the princess would now be known as Queen Victoria.

---

6. Maxwell, Sir Herbert, Bart. M.P., *Sixty Years a Queen* (Harmsworth Brothers Limited, 1897), p.3.

7. Ibid., p.4.

This painting by Henry Tanworth Wells depicts the Archbishop of Canterbury and Conyngham, the Lord Chancellor, informing Princess Victoria of her accession. It is worth noting that Conyngham's daughter, Lady Jane Churchill, would become one of Victoria's ladies of the bedchamber and a close friend and confidante until her death in 1900. (Public Domain)

Victoria was aware of the enormity of the responsibility that had been placed firmly upon her shoulders. Aged eighteen, she was the youngest British queen to ascend the throne and the first female sovereign since Queen Anne, who ruled 103 years earlier.

6

Oath to the Church of Scotland

This is the first official document that Victoria signed as sovereign at her first Privy Council meeting in the Red Saloon, Kensington Palace, on 20 June 1837.

The Oath to the Church of Scotland featured the signatures of the members of the Privy Council who attended that meeting. The document showed that Victoria was moving into a political role and that she was entering an environment that was entirely male dominated, with every signature, with the exception of her own, belonging to men. It also symbolised the beginning of her reign. More than 21,000 pieces of legislation was passed through Parliament and Victoria would have reviewed and personally authorised that legislature with her signature. Her letters and journal entries reveal that in private she would challenge, advise and counsel her ministers regarding policies and statutes passed through Parliament.

The Privy Council is a formal body of advisers to the sovereign comprising senior politicians and former members of the House of Commons and Lords appointed by the monarch. Its origins date back to the thirteenth century and its role is to advise the monarch on the conducting of duties, including the exercise of the Royal Prerogative and other protocols assigned to the sovereign by Acts of Parliament. Many of the powers of the Privy Council are ceremonial and relate to matters of constitutional importance. However, in Victoria's day and during the current reign of Elizabeth II the Privy Council is a vehicle for executive decisions presented by the Government which are then officially issued in the name of the sovereign. On 20 June 1837, Victoria was immediately emerged into matters of state and had to focus upon her responsibilities as monarch.

Her first task was to convene her first Privy Council Meeting. At 9 am Victoria received the Whig Prime Minister Viscount Melbourne in her private chambers alone. Melbourne's purpose was to brief her before the meeting. He would swiftly become an important adviser to Victoria, advising her on issues of government.

At 11 am Victoria went to the Red Saloon at Kensington Palace, where her ministers waited for her to arrive. The purpose of this meeting was for the Queen to appoint her Privy Councillors. Victoria was now Head of State and despite feeling solitary she maintained her confidence and composure as she entered the room alone, bowed to the Lords and then walked

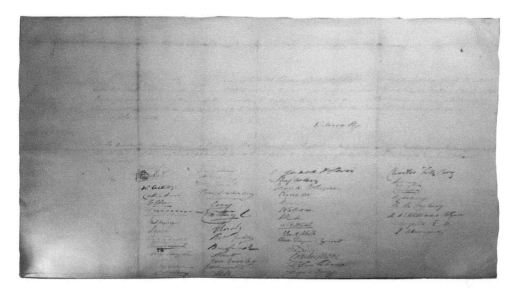

The Oath to the Church of Scotland was the first official document that Victoria signed as sovereign, an event that occurred during her first Privy Council Meeting in the Red Saloon at Kensington Palace. The document features the signatures of the attendees at that meeting. (The National Archives; EXT 9/35)

to her seat at the head of the table. Despite her inner apprehension, her sorrow for her late uncle and her nerves, she overcame these emotions.

The Queen recorded in her journal, 'I went in of course, quite alone and remained seated the whole time ... I was not at all nervous and had the satisfaction of hearing that people were satisfied with what I had done and how I had done it.'[8]

The members of the Privy Council were intrigued and curious about the young queen, but they soon became enamoured and assured by her firmness, confidence and abilities as she conducted her first Privy Council. Initial impressions were favourable. Duke of Wellington commented that, 'She not only filled her chair, she filled the room.'[9]

The oath that guaranteed the security of the Church of Scotland was the first document that Victoria signed as Queen. She then received the allegiance of the Privy Councillors present. The Dukes of Cumberland and Sussex, her uncles, were the first councillors to swear the oath of allegiance. Sussex was infirm and as he was about to kneel before Victoria to take the oath of allegiance, she anticipated his action, kissed his cheek and said with affection, 'Do not kneel, my uncle, for I am still Victoria, your niece.'[10]

8. Benson, Christopher & Esher, Viscount, *The Letters of Queen Victoria, A selection of from Her Majesty's correspondence between the years 1837 and 1861, Volume 1* (Published John Murray, London 1908), p.76.

9. Historic Royal Palaces website.

10. Wilson, Robert, *Life & Times of Queen Victoria, Vol. 1* (Cassell & Company Limited, London, 1887), p.21.

This painting by Sir David Wilkie depicts Victoria at the first Privy Council Meeting. Her uncles, the Dukes of Somerset and Sussex, are seated at the table. Viscount Melbourne stands before the Queen holding a pen in his right hand. Standing to his left is Lord Palmerston, the Foreign Secretary. The Duke of Wellington, former Prime Minister, is depicted in front of the right pillar. Sir Robert Peel, leader of the Conservative Party, the opposition, stands to his left. The Queen wore a black mourning dress, but Wilkie wanted her to stand out in the image among her privy councillors, who were wearing black, and to accentuate her innocence. It was for this reason that the Queen disliked this painting, describing it as 'one of the worst pictures I have ever seen, both as to painting and to likeness'. (Author's Collection)

The Duke of Wellington, Lord Palmerston, (the Foreign Secretary) and Sir Robert Peel were among those councillors who kissed the hand of the sovereign. Occasionally during the Privy Council meeting the Queen glanced towards Melbourne for guidance and assurance. During the early years of her reign, Melbourne mentored the Queen in politics. Alongside Leopold, King of Belgium, who guided her on the practicalities of sovereignty, both men would become paternal figures during her early reign as they filled the void left by her deceased father and offered impartial advice. Melbourne was provided with an apartment in Windsor Castle and rumours circulated that the Prime Minister, who was forty years her senior, was having a romantic affair with the Queen, but she regarded him as a father figure and the relationship was purely paternal.

7

St James's Palace, London

Proclamation of Queen Victoria in the courtyard of St James's Palace on 21 June 1837.

St James's Palace, built during the reign of Henry VIII, became the official residence of the sovereign in London and was used for state and ceremonial functions. In 1762, George III felt that the palace was unsuitable as a royal residence and bought Buckingham House for his wife, Queen Charlotte. Throughout the reigns of George III, George IV and William IV, St James's Palace continued to be used for ceremonial purposes. A state ball was held there to celebrate Princess Victoria's eighteenth birthday. Within a month she returned to St James's Palace on 21 June 1837 when she was proclaimed sovereign and this was her first appearance in public as queen. After Victoria ascended the throne, many court ceremonies were transferred to Buckingham Palace and St James's Palace ceased to be the primary royal residence in London.

The Privy Council ordered that Victoria should be proclaimed queen and this took place at St James's Palace on the following day, 21 June 1837. The purpose of the proclamation was to publicise and announce the accession. Vast crowds assembled outside St James's Palace in the courtyard to hear the proclamation read, but they did not expect the sovereign would be present. Victoria was escorted by a Guard of Honour comprising the Life Guards from Kensington Palace. On arrival at St James's Palace at ten o'clock, artillery in St James's Park and the Tower of London fired a salute. The Life Guards paraded in the courtyard. The Queen's Marshalmen, the Queen's Sergeant Trumpeter and the Household Drums and Trumpets, dressed in state uniforms, stood advance of the Life Guards. On the west side of the courtyard, beneath the window where Her Majesty stood, was the Sergeant at Arms on horseback bearing large gilt maces and heralds.

Victoria, attired in mourning dress, passed through the presence chamber, where she appeared at one of the windows that overlooked the large courtyard, supported by her mother, Viscount Melbourne and Lord Lansdowne, both dressed in state robes. The surprised crowd greeted the young queen with loud, jubilant cheers. A reporter recorded: 'Her Majesty looked extremely fatigued and pale, but returned the repeated cheers with which she was greeted with remarkable ease and dignity. She was dressed in deep mourning, with white tippet, white

The courtyard at St James's Palace has not changed in the 200 years since the proclamation of Queen Victoria. As the proclamation was read in the courtyard, Queen Victoria observed the ceremony from one of the windows on the balcony. (Author's Collection)

cuffs, and a border of white lace under a small black bonnet, which was placed far back on her head … Her Majesty seemed to view the proceedings with considerable interest.'[11]

The proclamation, which was issued at the first Privy Council meeting during the previous day, was read out by Sir William Woods (Clarenceaux King of Arms) acting as Deputy Garter, wearing a richly gold embroidered tabard.

After the proclamation had been read, the Queen entered the palace as the trumpets sounded 'God Save the Queen'. An article written in the *London Evening Standard* reported that the Queen was overcome by tears by the public reaction to her accession. Victoria gave audiences to Viscount Melbourne and various other officials before a second Privy Council in the Throne Room at St James's Palace, where those councillors who had not sworn the oath at Kensington Palace at the first Privy Council meeting during the previous day were sworn at this second meeting and a period of general mourning for William IV was ordered.

---

11. *Morning Advertiser*, 22 June 1837.

8

Victoria's Royal Arms

Victoria's life endangered when horses drawing her carriage bolted at Highgate on 6 July 1837.

The royal arms of Queen Victoria were presented to Mr Turner, the landlord of the Fox & Crown public house in Highgate, as a gift for restraining her horses, which bolted past his establishment down West Hill on 6 July 1837. Victoria's royal arms differed from her five predecessors. The arms were surmounted upon a lozenge instead of a shield because the sovereign was female; and the imperial crest of a lion surmounting a crown was removed as well as the arms of Hanover. The arms of Victoria consisted of four grand quarters representing England in the first and fourth quarters, and Scotland and Ireland in the Second and third quarters. These royal arms once adorned the Fox & Crown public house, West Hill, Highgate.

On 6 July 1837, two weeks after her accession, Victoria was taking a carriage ride with her mother to Highgate. The purpose of the trip to this village was to visit a royal servant who was ill. As she was returning to Kensington Palace down West Hill from Highgate, the four horses pulling her carriage lost control and they descended down this steep hill, placing the Queen and her mother in a perilous situation. The Fox & Crown public house, which was established during the reign of George III was located halfway down the hill. It was then known as the Fox under the Hill. Mr Turner, the landlord of the public house, realised the danger and at great risk to his own safety caught the reins, averting a catastrophe. A newspaper report, six decades after the incident, provided details of the moment when control of the carriage was lost close to the Fox & Crown:

> The royal ladies were brought into a situation of considerable danger, near the summit of the hill, which is exceedingly steep. This was occasioned by the pair of ponies [*sic* horses] which drew their chaise taking fright, and starting off rapidly downward. The landlord of the Fox & Crown, perceiving what had happened, ran into the road and seized the reins, bringing the animals to a stop, when the driver had lost control of them. He then assisted Her Majesty and the Duchess of Kent to alight, and conducted them into his house, and upstairs to the front room over the bar parlour, where they rested while some needful

The Royal Arms presented by Victoria to Mr Turner, landlord of the Fox & Crown, in 1837. It can be viewed by appointment at Highgate Literary and Science Institute, South Grove, Highgate. (Author's Collection)

Victoria's carriage was travelling down West Hill, Highgate, when her horses bolted and control of the carriage was lost. The Fox & Crown public house was positioned halfway down this hill on the right side of the road. (Author's Collection)

Above: The Fox & Crown on West Hill, Highgate, featuring Victoria's coat of arms displayed on the wall. (Author's Collection)

Right: The plaque on the wall of the building that today stands on the site of the Fox & Crown. (Author's Collection)

readjustment of the harness was made. At the same time, a wheelwright was sent for to examine the wheels, which had struck against the stone-curbing of the road, or against a post or some other royal obstacle. The favour of permission to display the royal arms, with the Crown supported by the Lion and the Unicorn, was granted to the tavern-keeper in acknowledgement of his assistance.

Victoria was alarmed by this dangerous situation, but relieved. She showed her gratitude by granting Mr Turner a licence for displaying these royal arms, which were displayed on the wall outside the Fox & Crown with the following inscription beneath:

THE FOX & CROWN, 6TH JULY 1837. This coat-of-arms is a grant from Queen Victoria for services rendered to Her Majesty while in danger travelling down this hill.

9

Buckingham Palace

Victoria became the first monarch to reside at Buckingham Palace as it became the official London residence of the sovereign.

Buckingham Palace looked completely different in 1837, when Victoria took residence, from how it looks today. Its name is derived from its previous owner, John Sheffield, the Duke of Buckingham, who commissioned the construction of a London home in 1703. It was transformed into a royal residence by George III when he purchased it in 1762. During the reign of George IV, Sir John Nash was commissioned to enlarge Buckingham House into a U-shaped building that enclosed a forecourt. A triumphal arch that Nash intended to celebrate the nation's victories at Trafalgar and Waterloo was erected at the entrance to Buckingham Palace and would be known as Marble Arch, which was later moved to its current position. The palace has 775 rooms, including 19 State rooms, 52 royal and guest bedrooms, 188 staff bedrooms, 78 bathrooms and 92 offices. George IV favoured Buckingham Palace but did not live to see the completion of Nash's work. His successor, William IV, detested it and preferred to reside at Clarence House. When Victoria relocated to Buckingham Palace on 13 July 1837, she became the first sovereign to rule from the palace and after the birth of the Princess Royal in 1840, it was not only the centre of Court and state affairs, it became the royal family home.

Approximately, £600,000 (worth £36 million in 2017) had been spent on renovating Buckingham Palace during the reign of George IV. However, when Victoria arrived in 1837, the work had not been completed and the palace had been unoccupied for twenty years. Soon after the funeral of William IV, and within three weeks of becoming sovereign, Victoria moved from Kensington Palace to Buckingham Palace, at 1.30 pm on 13 July 1837, in an open landau escorted by a troop of Lancers.

Victoria would use Buckingham Palace as a place to entertain dignitaries. On 10 May 1838, she held her first ball in Buckingham Palace, when Johann Strauss the elder and his orchestra performed Viennese waltzes in the Blue Drawing Room as her guests danced. Despite feeling reticent, she overcame her inhibitions and talked to her guests, dancing on two occasions during that evening.

Above: The distinctive façade of Buckingham Palace. (Courtesy of Leonid Andronov/Shutterstock)

Right: Victoria's private audience chamber photographed in 1900. (Library of Congress)

During the first eight years of her reign, Victoria gave birth to four of her nine children at Buckingham Palace but on 10 February 1845 she complained to Prime Minister Sir Robert Peel about the limited space within it to accommodate her expanding family and petitioned for it to be renovated. She wrote of:

the total want of accommodation for our little family, which is fast growing up. Any building must necessarily take some years before it can be safely inhabited. If it were to begin this autumn, it could hardly be occupied before the spring of 1848, when the

This painting by George Sidney Shepherd, entitled *Buckingham Palace, Her Majesty's Escort – 16th Lancers* and dated 1850, shows the palace after the renovations ordered by Victoria, including the removal of the triumphal arch and the construction of the east wing. The eastern façade of Buckingham Palace was remodelled in 1913. (Anne S.K. Brown Military Collection, Brown University Library)

Prince of Wales would be nearly seven, and the Princess Royal, nearly eight years old, and they cannot possibly be kept in the nursery any longer … Independent of this, most parts of the Palace are in a sad state, and will ere long require a further outlay to render them decent for the occupation of the royal family or any visitors the Queen may have to receive. A room, capable of containing a larger number of those persons whom the Queen has to invite in the course of the season to balls, concerts, etc. than any of the present apartments can at once hold, is much wanted.[12]

Peel was conscious of public opinion that had frowned upon the extravagance of George IV and was reluctant to commit public money to fund the renovations that Victoria was requesting. Edward Blore, the architect, was commissioned to produce a report on the state of Buckingham Palace and submit recommendations for a cost-effective plan to satisfy the Queen's request. On 13 August 1846, Parliament granted Victoria £20,000 (Worth £1.6 million in 2017) to start work on completing the refurbishments to Buckingham Palace, on the stipulation that Brighton Royal Pavilion was sold to offset part of the costs to fund the work. Blore was commissioned to design plans to construct a new wing that would connect the north and south wings, which would enclose the forecourt that had been built by Sir John Nash. By 1850 the East Wing had been constructed.

During the course of twenty-four years, from 1837 until 1861, Victoria had transformed Buckingham Palace, into the palace as it appears in the twenty-first century and converted it as a place of work, a centre of a bustling, provincial court and as a family home. The palace symbolised Victoria's role as a mother and her responsibilities of state as sovereign.

---

12. Benson, Vol. 2, op. cit., p.33.

10

Gold State Coach

Victoria used the Gold State Coach in the Coronation Procession to Westminster Abbey on 28 June 1838.

The Gold State Coach was used by Victoria for state occasions throughout her long reign. It has been used at every coronation since the crowning of George IV in 1821. Victoria mentioned her first use of the Gold State Carriage in her journal for the State Opening of Parliament on 20 November 1837 and again to the House of Lords on 23 December 1837, prior to her coronation in 1838.

Francis Hastings, 10th Earl of Huntingdon, the King's Master of the Horse, commissioned the construction of this gilded State Coach in 1760 for the coronation of George III and his wedding to Princess Charlotte of Mecklenburg-Strelitz in 1761. William Chambers designed the coach, while Giovanni Cipriani, the artist, painted the panels. The structure was sculptured by Joseph Wilton and the coach was gilded by Henry Pujolas. The cabin is supported by braces covered with Morocco leather and gilt buckles; and the interior is upholstered with satin and velvet.

The complexity of the design and structure meant that the team failed to meet the deadline for both the coronation of George III and his wedding. The State Coach was completed two years after the project was commissioned and first used by George III for the State Opening of Parliament on 25 November 1762. It has been used at every coronation since George IV was crowned King on 19 July 1821, including state openings of Parliament and the Coronation of Queen Victoria in 1838.

The State Carriage was drawn by eight cream-coloured horses on coronation day on 28 June 1838. Felix Mendelssohn, the composer, watched Victoria proceed to Westminster Abbey and wrote that the coach was 'golden and fairy-like, supported by Tritons with their tridents, and surmounted by the great crown of England'.[13] Although the Gold State Coach looked ornate and elaborate, it was uncomfortable to sit inside and Victoria complained of the 'distressing oscillation'.[14]

13. Baird, Julia, *Victoria the Queen, An Intimate Biography* (Blackfriars, 2016), p.76.

14. Anonymous, *Queen Elizabeth II and the Royal Family* (Dorling Kindersley Limited, London, 2016), p.137.

The gold State Coach used by Victoria during her coronation. (Shutterstock)

Victoria was welcomed with enthusiastic cheers from the multitude of people that lined the streets of London, who watched and enjoyed this spectacle of pomp and pageantry. The route of the coronation procession passed up Constitution Hill, through Piccadilly, down St James's Street, along Pall Mall, Cockspur Street, passing Charing Cross, Whitehall, Parliament Street and the Broad Sanctuary, arriving at the western entrance of Westminster Abbey at 11.30 am. The route was specifically designed to ensure that the Queen was visible to as many people as possible.

11

The Coronation Chair

Victoria crowned Queen at her coronation at Westminster Abbey on 28 June 1838.

The Coronation Chair was made under the orders of Edward I to enclose the Stone of Scone, which had been taken from Scotland and transferred to Westminster Abbey in 1296. It was built of oak and completed in 1301. This throne was used during the coronation of thirty-eight English monarchs including the Coronation ceremony of Queen Victoria on 28 June 1838. In her journal, Victoria referred to the Coronation Chair as St Edward's Chair.

Victoria arrived at the west entrance of Westminster Abbey on the day of her coronation at 11.30 am, where she was received by the Archbishop of Canterbury, William Howley, marking the beginning of the ceremony that would last for five hours. Her train was carried by the daughters of eight peers as the Queen proceeded through the aisle towards a faldstool in the centre of the choir. On approaching the faldstool, the Queen saw the Coronation Chair. Lady Wilhelmina Stanhope, one of the trainbearers, later recalled:

> I think her heart fluttered a little as we reached the throne; at least, the colour mounted to her cheeks, brow and even neck, and her breath came quickly. However, the slight emotion she showed was very transient, and she stood perfectly motionless while the Archbishop, in an almost inaudible voice, proclaimed her our undoubted Sovereign.[15]

'The Anointing' was the part of the ceremony, when Victoria sat upon the Coronation Chair, while four Knights of the Garter held a cloth canopy of gold above her head. The Dean of Westminster took the ampulla from the altar and poured an aromatic holy oil upon the anointing spoon, which was used by the Archbishop of Canterbury to anoint the head, hands and chest of the Queen, marking them with the cross and asserting the declaration, 'Be thou anointed with holy oil, as kings, priests and prophets were anointed.' A prayer was then said before the choir sang the British anthem 'Zadok the Priest' composed by the German composer George Frederick Handel originally for the coronation of George II in

---

15. Lorne, Marquis of, *V.R.I. Her Life and Empire* (Harmsworth Bros Ltd., 1902), p.89.

The Coronation Chair in Westminster Abbey. (Copyright: Dean and Chapter of Westminster)

1727. The investiture began with the Queen dressed in coronation robes. The Jewelled Sword of Offering and Sovereign's Orb was presented to the Queen before being placed upon the altar. The Investiture was concluded with the delivery of the Ring and Sceptre. The ring was placed on the fourth finger of her right hand. After being presented with the regalia of State, the new State Crown, which was adapted from the one used by William IV, was placed upon the Sovereign's head as she sat on the Coronation Chair. Victoria recalled the moment when she was crowned:

I was then seated upon St. Edward's chair, where the Dalmatic robe was clasped round me by the great Lord Chamberlain. Then followed all the various things; and last (of those things) the Crown being placed on my head – which was, I must own, a most beautiful, impressive moment: all the Peers and Peeresses put on their coronets at the same instant. My excellent Lord Melbourne, who stood very close to me throughout the whole ceremony, was completely overcome at this moment, and very much affected; he gave me such a kind, and I say fatherly look, the shouts, which were very great,

The coronation of Queen Victoria in Westminster Abbey, 28 June 1838. (Anne S.K. Brown Military Collection, Brown University Library)

the drums, the trumpets, the firing of the guns, all at the same instant, rendered the spectacle most imposing.[16]

As the crown was placed upon Victoria's head, the sun's rays shone upon her face and diamonds on her crown reflected those rays to create a halo around her head. Harriett Martineau was present at the coronation and recalled: 'gleams of the sun slanted into the Abbey and presently travelled down to the peeresses. I had never before seen the full effect of diamonds. As the light travelled each peeress shone like a rainbow. The brightness, vastness and dreamy magnificence of the scene produced a strange effect of exhaustion and sleepiness.'[17]

At the moment the crown was placed upon Victoria's head an artillery salute was fired from the Tower of London and St James's Park and Westminster Abbey echoed with loud cheers, trumpets and beating drums. Lady Wilhelmina Stanhope recalled: 'The burst of applause in the Abbey when the crown was placed on her head and the sight of all the peers and peeresses crowning themselves at the same moment was really most impressive; and in the midst of the cheering Handel's magnificent anthem, "The Queen shall rejoice!" thundered in.'[18]

---

16. Benson, Vol. 1, op. cit., pp.121–3.

17. Ball, Frederick T., *Queen Victoria: Scenes and Incidents of Her Life and Reign* (A.G. Watson, Toronto, Canada, 1888), pp.68–9.

18. Lorne, op. cit., p.90.

12

The Royal Pavilion

Victoria stayed at the Royal Pavilion, Brighton, during Christmas 1838.

Construction of the Royal Pavilion at Brighton as a seaside residence for George, Prince of Wales, began in 1787. As Prince Regent, he commissioned John Nash to renovate and extend the Royal Pavilion and transform it into an exotic oriental palace fusing Regency design with Indian influences featuring domes and minarets. Work began in 1815 and was completed in 1822. The Royal Pavilion symbolised the decadent extravagances that would tarnish the reputation of the monarchy under Victoria's uncle, George IV.

Victoria visited Brighton for the first time as sovereign on 5 October 1837. In preparation for her visit, the streets were festooned with continuous lights along the streets. From balconies her name 'Victoria' was formed in flowers, and there were also signs expressing the loyalty of the inhabitants of Brighton, displaying the words 'Welcome, Victoria'; 'Victoria our Queen';

The Royal Pavilion in Brighton. (Author's Collection)

The Banqueting Room at the Royal Pavilion in Brighton from John Nash's *Views of the Royal Pavilion* (1826), archive of the Brighton Pavilion.

'Victoria, long may she reign'; and 'Victoria, our beloved Queen'. Crowds thronged upon the seaside resort to join the local residents to welcome her arrival.

Victoria was not enamoured by the Royal Pavilion and before her next visit during Christmas 1838 she wrote of her dislike of the house. She felt uncomfortable due to its association with George IV. The Royal Pavilion lacked privacy, which was further exacerbated by the advent of the railway that made Brighton accessible to the seaside resort in Sussex. Brighton became crowded, which made the Queen loathe the town. Victoria wrote that 'the people here are very indiscreet and troublesome'.[19] George IV built the Royal Pavilion, not for the purposes of raising a family, but as a pleasure palace by the sea, so as Victoria's family increased, the house could not accommodate her children and was eventually deemed unsuitable as a family home. As mentioned previously, Victoria received a grant from Parliament to fund the refurbishment and expansion of Buckingham Palace in 1846 on the condition that she sold the Royal Pavilion to offset some of that expense. The process of transferring furnishings and interior decorations to Buckingham Palace began during that same year. In 1850, the Royal Pavilion was eventually sold to the town of Brighton for £53,000 (£4 million in 2017).

---

19. *Brighton & Hove Independent*, 25 December 2014.

13

Medal Commemorating Victoria's Marriage to Albert

Victoria proposed to Prince Albert on 15 October 1839.

Against the wishes of William IV, King Leopold of Belgium, encouraged a romance to flourish between his niece Victoria and nephew Prince Albert of Saxe-Coburg in 1836 after he instigated a meeting between them at Kensington Palace. Although Victoria enjoyed his company, she was not ready to commit to marriage. It was not until October 1839, when Prince Albert visited Windsor Castle, that Victoria fell in love with her German cousin and within days they were engaged. The *London Gazette* is one of the official journals of the British Government and is used to notify the nation of royal events. A notice was published in it to announce the betrothal between Victoria and Albert. This medal was produced to commemorate the event.

By 1839, Victoria had been on the throne for nearly two years and there was considerable pressure placed upon her to marry and produce an heir, much to her dismay. Her feelings towards Albert began to change when he visited Windsor Castle on 10 October 1839. The purpose of his visit was to ascertain whether there was any likelihood of romance and marriage with the British sovereign. If the answer was yes, he was willing to keep himself free from other suitors. He did not have long to wait to learn of Victoria's feelings towards him, for she could not resist the handsome features of the German prince and his impeccable manners. She wrote: 'Albert's beauty is most striking and he is so amiable and unaffected – in short, very fascinating; he is excessively admired here.'[20]

Within three days, on 13 October, Victoria confided in Melbourne that she confirmed that he was a suitable choice for marriage. He advised her to wait another week before confirming her decision. She did not take Melbourne's advice and decided to propose to Albert. It was a delicate situation for both Victoria and Albert because protocol dictated that Albert could not propose to her, despite his interest in marriage. Given that Victoria was sovereign, the first advances and proposal should be instigated by her. On 14 October she informed Melbourne that she was going to marry Albert, and he expressed his encouragement and support.

20. Benson, Vol. 1, op. cit., p.188.

Above left and above right: The front and rear of the commemorative medal produced following Victoria's marriage to Prince Albert, which was announced in *The London Gazette* on 23 November 1839. (Author's Collection)

Victoria invited Albert into her Private Audience Chamber at Windsor Castle during the following day, 15 October. She recalled: 'At half-past twelve I sent for Albert. He came to the closet where I was alone. After a few moments I said to him that I thought he must be aware why I wished him to come, and that it would make me happy if he would consent to what I wished (namely to marry me). There was no hesitation on his part, but the offer was received with the greatest demonstration of kindness and affection. He is perfection in every way – in beauty, in everything. I told him I was quite unworthy of him. He said he would be very happy to spend his life with me.'[21]

Their engagement remained a secret for a month until 23 November 1839, when Victoria announced her betrothal to her Privy Council at Buckingham Palace. After her declaration, Lord Lansdowne stood up and asked on behalf of the Privy Council, that the good news might be printed. The Queen gave her consent and this notice was published in the *London Gazette* during that day.

---

21. Lorne, op. cit., p.110.

14

Salmon & Gluckstein Cigarette Card Depicting Victoria Wearing her Wedding Dress

Salmon & Gluckstein were a British-based tobacconist, established in 1873 by Samuel Gluckstein and Barnett Salmon. They declared themselves 'pioneers of the smoking world', with 140 retail outlets in Britain. A series of six cigarette cards were produced in 1897 depicting Victoria at various stages of her life. This card depicts Victoria on her wedding day. She made white highly fashionable and established the custom of the white wedding in Britain that is prevalent to this day.

Victoria is credited to have installed the tradition of the white wedding, where the bride wore white, and the founding of a tradition and an industry that flourishes today in Britain and around the world. Previous royal brides had favoured blue or black, but Victoria insisted that her dress be coloured white in order to ensure that the public could clearly see her during the procession from Buckingham Palace to St James's Palace on the wedding day.

Victoria was also responsible for establishing the royal wedding as a public celebration to be enjoyed by the nation, instead of a private ceremony. The nation was undergoing tough times politically and this wedding aimed to be positive, raise public morale and deflect from those problems

The Salmon & Gluckstein cigarette card that depicts Victoria as a bride. (Author's Collection)

occurring in Britain. Charles Dickens, the eminent Victorian author, succumbed to the positivity that Victoria brought to the monarchy and wrote, 'Society is unhinged here by Her Majesty's marriage and I am sorry to say that I have fallen hopelessly in love with the Queen.'[22]

Brussels lace was in fashion when Victoria was planning her nuptials, however she bought Honiton lace for the material for her wedding dress, a move that would promote the British lace industry, especially in Honiton, Devon. She further championed her nation's commerce by commissioning English (Spitalfields) silk to make the dress. Albert designed a coronet for her to wear as a wedding present, but the Queen decided to wear a headdress of orange blossoms at the ceremony. She also wore her Turkish diamond neckless and earrings, together with a sapphire broach that was given to her by Albert as a gift. The *Tipperary Free Press* described the Queen's wedding dress:

> Her Majesty the Queen wore on her head a wreath orange blossom and veil of Honiton lace, with a necklace and earrings of diamonds. Her Majesty's dress was of white satin, with a deep trimming of Honiton lace, design similar to that of the veil. The body and sleeves were richly trimmed with the same material to correspond. The train was of white satin, and was also lined with white satin, trimmed with orange blossoms (white). The cost of the lace on the Queen's drew was 1,000l. The satin was a pure white. Her Majesty wore an armlet having the motto of the Order of the Garter, 'Honi soit mal y pense', inscribed, and also wore the star of the Order. The lace which formed the flounce of the dress measures four yards, and is three-quarters of a yard in depth.[23]

Immediately before midday on 10 February 1840, Victoria's carriage passed through the gates and the arch of Buckingham Palace. Despite the heavy rain, the crowds gave an enormous cheer as her cortège left Buckingham Palace in a procession along the Mall towards St James's Palace. Approximately, 50,000 spectators, hoping to get a glimpse of the royal bride and bridegroom, had assembled in the slight rain since 6 am along the route and despite the inclement weather they cheered enthusiastically as the Queen passed. Many of the spectators climbed trees in order to gain a more favourable place to view the procession pass through the Mall, but some tree branches broke because of the weight. Victoria was overwhelmed by the response of the crowd. She wrote:

> Independent of my great personal happiness, the reception we both met with yesterday was the most gratifying and enthusiastic I have ever experienced; there was no end of the crowds in London, and all along the road.[24]

22. Knight, Alfred E., *The Life & Reign of the Queen* (S.W. & Partridge & Co., London, 1896), p.98.

23. *Tipperary Free Press*, 15 February 1840.

24. Benson, Vol. 1, op. cit., p.217.

15

Chapel Royal Window, St James's Palace

Victoria married Prince Albert of Saxe-Coburg in the Chapel Royal.

The building of St James's Palace was completed during the reign of Henry VIII in 1540. Exactly three hundred years later, the marriage ceremony of Victoria and Albert took place in the Chapel Royal within St James's Palace in front of five hundred distinguished guests.

On entering the Chapel Royal at noon on 10 February 1840, the flourish trumpets ceased and the organ began to play the National Anthem, as Victoria was walked up the aisle by the Duke of Sussex, her favourite uncle. Victoria was led into the Chapel Royal by Melbourne, who carried the Sword of State, symbolising the monarch's power and authority. Twelve bridesmaids, wearing white dresses and white roses, following behind the bride carried her train. Lady Wilhelmina Stanhope, who was one of the bridesmaids, recalled: 'The Queen was perfectly composed and quiet, but unusually pale. She walked very slowly, giving ample time for all the spectators to gratify their curiosity, and certainly she was never before more earnestly scrutinised.'[25]

Albert was standing at the altar, wearing the uniform of a British field marshal, adorned with the insignia of the Garter and jewels presented to him by the Queen. The names of the bride and bridegroom were mentioned without titles, simply 'Victoria' and 'Albert'. The Archbishop of Canterbury had asked her if she wanted the promise 'to obey' her husband removed from the wedding vows in the ceremony, but she declined. The queen of the largest empire in the world promised to 'obey' and serve as well as to love and honour the man to whom her troth was plighted. The ceremony lasted thirty minutes and at the end, the two field trains of Royal Artillery stationed in St James's Park and at the Tower of London fired a final salute at 12.30 pm and all the church bells in London rung, announcing that the wedding ceremony had concluded. The royal couple then adjourned to the Throne Room, where the signing of the registers took place.

---

25. Lorne, op. cit., p.110.

The entrance to St James's Palace and the exterior window of the Chapel Royal (the one on the right) where Victoria married Albert on 10 February 1840. (Author's Collection)

Before leaving St James's Palace, the Queen gave her twelve bridesmaids a turquoise eagle broach as a gift. The newly wedded couple returned to Buckingham Palace for the wedding breakfast, before their journey to Windsor Castle, where they were to spend their honeymoon. On 11 February 1840, the day after the wedding, Victoria wrote of her joy and happiness to Leopold. 'My Dearest Uncle, I write to you from here, the happiest, happiest Being that ever existed. Really, I do not think it possible for anyone in the world to be happier, or as happy as I am. He is an Angel, and his kindness and affection for me is really touching. To look in those dear eyes, and that dear sunny face, is enough to make me adore him. What I can do to make him happy is my greatest delight … I was a good deal tired last night, but am quite well again today, and happy.'[26]

As a younger woman, she was passionate, romantic with her husband, whom she adored and idolised. While on honeymoon they could enjoy moments of intimacy, they shared a bed and saw each other in their underclothes. On the third day of her honeymoon, Victoria wrote in her journal that Albert helped her put on her stockings. Committed and dedicated to her role as sovereign, the honeymoon lasted only three days as she had to return to Buckingham Palace on 14 February 1840 to deal with affairs of state.

26. Benson, Vol. 1, op. cit., p.217.

16

Penny Black Stamp

The world's first pre-paid adhesive postage stamp used in a public postal system was officially released on 6 May 1840 bearing Victoria's image.

As the British became more literate during the nineteenth century, there was an increase in sending letters and a great demand for a uniform postal service. However, the postal charges in 1837 depended upon the number of sheets within the letter and the distance travelled, which made the cost of delivery complex and expensive. The recipient was expected to pay for the charge of delivery. Peers, Members of Parliament and Cabinet Ministers had the right of franking, which meant that by writing their names on the outside of their own letters or the letters of family and friends they could enjoy the privilege of free postage. This privilege was open to abuse on a grand scale where many affluent people sent letters for free. It meant the Post Office was losing revenue and that those on low incomes were subsidising the wealthy. This prompted Rowland Hill, Secretary to the Postmaster General, to produce a paper entitled 'Post Office Reform: Its Importance and Practicality', which promoted the concept of postage at a low, uniform rate, based on weight and it would be prepaid. Hill's plan was to reduce the average charge of six penny to one penny for each stamp, on an adhesive label, and that would be a uniform charge for delivery of any letter to any destination in Britain irrespective of distance. It took two years for Hill to convince Parliament and the public that his proposal was commercially viable and would reduce postage rates. The Postage Act was passed in the Houses of Parliament on 17 August 1839 to implement Hill's proposals for regulation and reform.

A competition to design the stamp was announced by Hill, but despite receiving 2,600 entries, none were deemed suitable. Hill decided that the stamp should feature the Queen's head, which would be difficult to forge. The image used depicted a young Victoria, taken from an engraving produced by Charles Heath, after a sketch drawn by Henry Corbould that was based on a sculpture by William Wyon for the City Medal that commemorated her visit to the City of London in November 1837.

This image of Victoria would remain on British stamps throughout her reign. The Penny Black set a precedent for all British stamps to feature a portrait of the monarch within the design. British stamps since the reign of Victoria are the only stamps in the world not to indicate the country of origin, because the sovereign's image epitomises Britain.

A mint block of thirty Penny Black stamps.

The Uniform Penny Post was inaugurated on 1 May 1840 and enabled the secure, expedient and inexpensive method of delivery of letters, but the Penny Black was not validated until 6 May. All free postage policies were abolished, which meant that Members of Parliament and Victoria had to pay for the postage of a letter. Five days later, postage could be prepaid with the first postage stamp, known as the Penny Black.

The Penny Black was an adhesive stamp that prepaid postage, allowing the delivery of letters of weight up to ½oz to be delivered as a standard rate of one penny, irrespective of distance. There were two versions, including one that was used by the general public that included an image of the Queen and four Maltese Crosses in each corner. A second version was produced specifically for office use known as the 'VR issue', which was similar to the other version except that the Maltese Crosses were repaved with the letter's 'V' and 'R'.

The Penny Post had revolutionised the postal service and encouraged increased volumes of postage throughout Victoria's reign. In 1837, 80,000 letters and 44,000 newspapers were delivered by the Post Office, amounting to a total of 124,000 items. During a twelve-month period in 1895–96, postal deliveries, excluding telegrams, had increased to 3,031,553,196 items, producing a profit amounting to £30,315,532.[27]

In 1840 when the Penny Black was introduced, there were two methods of posting a letter. The sender could take a letter to a receiving house, the precursor to a post office, where it would enter the national postal network prior to delivery. Alternatively, the sender could hand it to a uniformed bellman, who walked the streets collecting letters from the public. The bellman derived the name because he rang a bell to alert people of his presence.

---

27. Maxwell, op. cit., p.25.

17

Constitution Hill

First Assassination attempt on Victoria by Edward Oxford.

On 10 June 1840, at 6.15 pm Victoria left Buckingham Palace by the Garden Gate entrance in an open carriage with Albert to visit her mother, the Duchess of Kent, at her residence in Belgrave Square. The royal couple went on an early evening drive before dinner to Hyde Park at the same time regularly for the past fortnight. As they were passing halfway along Constitution Hill towards Hyde Park Corner, Edward Oxford fired two shots at Victoria. After firing the first shot, the Queen stood up, but Albert, who was in the carriage, pulled her down to take cover just before Oxford fired the second.

As the carriage carrying Victoria and Albert proceeded swiftly along Constitution Hill towards Hyde Park Corner, a female was seen trying to restrain Oxford by the skirt of his coat, inside the railings of Green Park, 8 yards from where Oxford fired at the

A view of Constitution Hill, where Edward Oxford attempted to assassinate Victoria. (Author's Collection)

A print depicting the assassination attempt made by Edward Oxford on Victoria as she rode in a carriage with Albert on Constitution Hill on 10 June 1840. (Library of Congress)

Queen. Arthur Lowe and William Clayton rushed towards Oxford to apprehend him. Mr Beckham, a Page of Honour to the Queen, and another bystander, Josiah Wright, also challenged the assassin. After some resistance they overwhelmed Oxford and seized one pistol from his hand and another concealed in the breast of his coat, before police constables Charles Brown and Charles Smith from the Metropolitan Police arrived to arrest him. Oxford said to Brown, 'I shall go quietly with you – I did it.'[28] A man named Pecks testified in a police report:

I have been in London for about a week from Dorsetshire, and have never seen the Queen. I was anxious to see her, and accordingly I went to the park and placed myself near the palace; after being there for a few minutes I saw Her Majesty and Prince Albert come out of the Palace, but not obtaining a good view, I ran on to Green Park, turning around by the single road by the angle to the west road. I placed myself about forty yards in the road towards Hyde Park, for I had never seen the Queen before, and I therefore had a quite desire to see her. On her coming up, I consider that there were not nine people

28. *The Evening Chronicle*, 12 June 1840.

present: the prisoner [Edward Oxford] was standing near me, he had his hands folded across under his coat. As the carriage came within a few yards of him, I saw him take his right arm from the left side of his coat, and pulling out a pistol he fired it. He held it as if he was fighting a duel or point blank. I thought it was an act of rejoicing, but instantly afterwards he drew a second pistol from his breast. He then crossed his hands, and stooped as if he took aim, and then fired. The instant he did so, Prince Albert looked very flushed in his face, but the Queen appeared to me not to change countenance, for she leapt forward and spoke to Prince Albert, and he then drove off rapidly towards Hyde Park. I became alarmed, and not knowing what was meant ran away. On my reaching Covent Garden, I told a constable what I had seen, who took me to his inspector, and came here with me … I had a very good view of the Queen, and she appeared by no means alarmed when the pistols were fired.

In order not to alarm the Duchess of Kent, Albert insisted that they should proceed to the home of Victoria's mother, who would have certainly found out about the incident. Their journey was brief, and only to reassure the Duchess of Kent that her daughter was safe, and they returned to Buckingham Palace at 7.15 pm. They were escorted by an enthusiastic and supportive crowd during that journey.

Edward Oxford was employed in the Hog-in-the-Pound public house in Marylebone Lane near Oxford Street, as a pot boy. He was reported to be aged seventeen or eighteen in various newspapers. He was charged 'with maliciously and unlawfully discharging two pistols at the Queen and Prince Albert'. He was sent to trial at the Old Bailey, where he pleaded 'not guilty' to the charge of 'traitorously and maliciously shooting at Her Majesty the Queen'. Oxford was declared insane and committed to a lunatic asylum.

On 30 May 1842, John Francis made a second attempt to assassinate Victoria, close to where Oxford fired from. William Hamilton, also attempted to assassinate Victoria on Constitution Hill close to the attempts made by Oxford and Francis on 19 May 1849. Victoria was never intimidated by attempts to assassinate her and continued to go about her everyday business, including daily rides in her carriage through London, throughout her reign.

18

Lily Font used for the Christening of the Princess Royal

Victoria's first child, Princess Victoria, was christened in the Throne Room at Buckingham Palace on 10 February 1841. The Lily Font is depicted in this engraving.

Victoria, Princess Royal, known as Vicky, or 'Pussy' or 'Pussette', Victoria's first child, was born on 21 November 1840. Albert would have preferred a son, for Victoria wrote, 'For a moment only was he disappointed at its being a daughter and not a son.'[29] Albert would be the doting father and cared for his wife as she recovered from the trauma of her first pregnancy. Victoria wrote to Leopold on 15 December 1840: 'Your little grand-niece is most flourishing; she gains daily in health, strength and, I may add, beauty; I think she will be very like her dearest father; she grows amazingly; I shall be proud to present her to you'.[30]

Before the Princess Royal was christened, Victoria learned that she was pregnant again and on the day before the christening Albert nearly drowned while skating on the ice in the lake in Buckingham Palace Gardens. He assisted Victoria across the ice to the island on 9 February 1841 and skated around the island once before the ice cracked and he was submerged in water up to his neck. Victoria stretched out her arms to stop him from going under the surface and assisted him out of the lake.

Victoria and Albert commissioned E. and W. Smith, procurers of domestic plate to the royal family, for the production of a new baptismal font. The firm sub-contracted this order to Barnard & Co., who created this font that featured an enlarged flower, bordered by water lilies and leaves, which is surmounted upon a stem flanked by three seated cherubs at the base, upon a circular plinth decorated with coats of arms. Water lilies were incorporated into the design because they symbolised purity and new life. After completion, Barnard & Co. presented a bill for £189 9s 4d. (worth £11,500 in 2017). Except for the christening of the Prince of Wales in 1842, when the Charles II font was used, the Lily Font has been used at every royal christening since 1841.

The christening took place in the Throne Room at Buckingham Palace during the afternoon on 10 February 1841 on Victoria and Albert's first wedding anniversary. This illustration depicts the christening, showing Victoria dressed in a white silk gown, which was trimmed

---

29. Knight, op. cit., p.112.

30. Benson, Vol. 1, op. cit., p.251.

Above left: A depiction of the christening of the Princess Royal, featuring the Lily Font. (Anne S.K. Brown Military Collection, Brown University Library)

Above right: Victoria with the infant Princess Victoria on her lap. (Courtesy of the Wellcome Collection)

with her wedding lace, wearing her diamond diadem, while Albert was dressed in the uniform of a field marshal. The christening ceremony was conducted by the Archbishop of Canterbury in the presence of her mother, her uncles, King Leopold and the Duke of Sussex and the Duke of Wellington. The Archbishop used water from the River Jordan to christen the baby, who was named Victoria, Adelaide, Mary Louise. Prince Albert described the ceremony in a letter to his grandmother, the Dowager Duchess of Gotha, written on 12 February 1841:

> The christening had gone off very well. Your little great-grandchild behaved with great propriety, and like a Christian. She was awake, but did not cry at all, and seemed to crow with immense satisfaction and the lights and brilliant uniforms, for she is very intelligent and observing. The ceremony took place at half-past 6 pm; and after it there was a dinner, and then we had some instrumental music. The health of the little one was drunk with great enthusiasm.[31]

The Princess Royal was betrothed to Prince Frederick of Prussia aged sixteen and married in 1858. On 9 March 1888, her husband became Emperor Frederick III, but her tenure as Empress of Russia lasted ninety days when he died on 15 June 1888 and was succeeded by their son, William II. Victoria lived for sixty years until she died of breast cancer on 13 August 1901, eight months after the death of her mother.

---

31. Jago, Dr. Kurt, *Letters of the Prince Consort 1831 – 1861* (John Murray, London, 1938). p.72.

19

Two Dry Docks, Woolwich

Victoria and Albert watched the launch of HMS *Trafalgar* at the Royal Dockyard, Woolwich, on 21 June 1841.

Since its establishment in 1512 during the reign of Henry VIII, Woolwich had been an important dockyard for the Royal Navy and that tradition continued three hundred years later into the reign of Victoria. Warships continued to be built at Woolwich Dockyard and it was here that she would embark on her royal yacht HMY *Albert and Victoria* for visits to Scotland and Northern Europe. Two dry docks that originate from the Kings Yard, which was expanded during Henry VIII's reign in 1540 and used during the Victorian era, still exist on the south bank of the River Thames at Woolwich.

On 21 June 1841, Victoria and Albert watched the launch of HMS *Trafalgar* at Woolwich Dockyard. The building under which *Trafalgar*, a 120-gun first-rate ship of the line, had been constructed was decorated with standards of the royal crown, along with numerous Union Jacks and a single flag adorned by the arms of Saxe-Coburg and Gotha.

The Queen was welcomed by enormous crowds that lined both embankments and 30,000 sightseers on approximately fifty steamers that had assembled on the River Thames at Woolwich positioned close to the launch site. Tragedy occurred minutes before the launch ceremony when a skiff containing four men, four women and a waterman who was rowing them, collided with a fishing boat. The skiff capsized and the entire party fell into the water. The upturned skiff went under a barge and a sailing boat and knocked several other spectators into the river. The strong currents carried these people along the River Thames and the many boats that were in the vicinity saved everyone except for two individuals who drowned.[32]

Lieutenant Rivers, who had lost an arm during the Battle of Trafalgar, was in command of 100 Greenwich Pensioners, veterans from the battle, who were invited to take part in the launching ceremony. They were all assembled on the poop deck of the vessel as it was launched.

A gun salute at 2.30 pm heralded the commencement of the launching ceremony. At Victoria's insistence, Lady Bridport, niece of Vice Admiral Lord Nelson, was given the honour

---

32. *John Bull*, 26 June 1841.

Two Tudor docks survive at Woolwich. This is the eastern dock looking south towards the River Thames. These docks were used during the reign of Victoria to build ships for the Royal Navy. (Author's Collection)

of launching HMS *Trafalgar*, with a bottle of wine that was aboard HMS *Victory* during the Battle of Trafalgar, which according to tradition was broke on the bows of the ship when she received her name. Victoria watched the launching from a viewing stand built adjacent to the dock, as the majestic vessel glided into the water amidst the cheers of the onlookers. After entering 150 yards into the River Thames, its anchor was dropped and the band played 'Rule Britannia'. The Queen was going to embark upon the *Firebrand* to view HMS *Trafalgar* after its launch, but heavy rain fell, which meant that she abandoned that plan and returned to Buckingham Palace.

Victoria would frequently use Woolwich Dockyard for beginning and ending passages aboard her royal yachts. She departed from Woolwich aboard HMY *Royal George* on 29 August 1842 for her first visit to Scotland and used the dock during the successive years for her annual excursions to Scotland. In 1843 she visited her uncle, King Leopold, and toured Belgium including visits to Ostend, Bruges, Ghent, Brussels and Antwerp. She ended this tour at Woolwich on 21 September 1843, disembarking from her new yacht HMY *Victoria and Albert*.

20

St George's Chapel, Windsor

The Prince of Wales is christened.

Edward IV commenced building St George's Chapel, within Windsor Castle, in 1475. The nave and stone vaulted ceiling were constructed by Henry VII and Henry VIII completed the work in 1528. Victoria's forebears Edward IV, Henry VIII, Charles I and her father, the Duke of Kent, were buried within St George's Chapel and it was here on 25 January 1842 that her second child and heir, Edward, Prince of Wales, was christened. Later during her reign, five of Victoria's children would marry in St George's Chapel and in 1901 her funeral service was held here. Her coffin was kept here for two nights before her interment at the Royal Mausoleum, Frogmore.

A year after the birth of Princess Victoria, on 9 November 1841, Albert Edward, known as Bertie, was born at Buckingham Palace. Victoria confirmed in her diary that she suffered severely during the birth, which left her exhausted. She found each pregnancy difficult and it would affect her physically and emotionally. Two weeks after giving birth to her second child, Victoria revealed in her journal that she felt fatigued and depressed. She also confirmed in a letter to Leopold that she had 'been suffering so from lowness that it made me quite miserable'.[33] Despite the trauma she was pleased to have given birth to a healthy son. She wrote to Leopold, 'Our little boy is a wonderfully strong and large child, with large dark blue eyes, a finely formed but somewhat large nose, and a pretty little mouth; I hope and pray he may be like his dearest Papa.'[34]

On 4 December, Bertie was proclaimed Prince of Wales. Although he was her second child, he was her first son, which meant that he passed over Vicky, her older daughter, to become the first in line and heir to the throne.

The christening of the Prince of Wales took place at St George's Chapel at Windsor Castle on 25 January 1842 in a ceremony officiated over by the Archbishop of Canterbury. Three hundred distinguished guests were invited to attend, but heavy snow prevented many from attending. Frederick William IV, King of Prussia, was among the guests who were present. The First Battalion, Grenadier Guards, provided the Guard of Honour. The Lord Chamberlain had provided tickets for members of the public to gain access to the Lower Ward of Windsor

33. Benson, Vol. 1, op. cit., p.366.

34. Ibid., p.364.

St George's Chapel, Windsor Castle. (Courtesy of Aurelien Guichard)

Castle to see the royal procession. It was reported that 'the infant Prince, a fine healthy-looking babe, was carried in the arms of the nurse, Mrs Brough, who held him up in the carriage so that he might be seen by the public. The moment he was seen by the crowd, there was a loud and general cheer, which was kept up along the entire line of the procession. The Queen and Prince Albert followed. Her Majesty and her Illustrious Consort experienced a loyal and enthusiastic greeting, which they acknowledged by repeatedly bowing to the crowd.'[35]

Bertie was dressed in the robe made for his elder sister Vicky's christening and this was used for all successive christenings of Victoria's children. The ceremony was conducted with pomp and splendour, with specially brought from the River Jordan for the occasion. A raised platform had been placed in front of the altar upon which was placed the ancient font traditionally used to baptise Princes of Wales since the reign of Charles II. This font had been moved from the Tower of London to St George's Chapel, where it had been re-gilt for this special occasion.

Victoria entered St George's Chapel attired in the robe of Sovereign of the Garter over a velvet crimson dress. She wore the collar of the Order over her shoulder and its star on her left breast. On her head was the diamond tiara. The Duke of Wellington, in his capacity as Leader of the House of Lords, stood behind the Queen's chair holding the Sword of State during the ceremony. The Halleluiah chorus reverberated through the chapel before the Archbishop gave the blessing. Victoria wrote of the impressive spectacle of holding the christening in St George's Chapel: 'How impossible it is to describe how beautiful and imposing the effect of the whole scene was in the fine old chapel, with the banners and music, and the light shining upon the altar.'[36]

---

35. *Monmouthshire Beacon*, 29 January 1842.

36. Lorne, op. cit., p.134.

21

The Mall

Further assassination attempts upon Victoria's life on 29 May and 3 July 1842.

Another assassination attempt took place two years after the first. It happened on 29 May 1842, when Victoria and Albert were returning from the Chapel Royal at St James's Palace. As their carriage proceeded towards Buckingham Palace along the Mall near to Stafford House (now known as Lancaster House), John Francis, a carpenter's son, stepped from the crowd and fired a shot at the royal party. Fortunately, the shot misfired, although Albert thought he saw and heard it. The Queen was on the other side of the carriage and continued to acknowledge the crowds. Albert asked, 'Did you hear that? I may be mistaken, but I am sure that I saw someone take aim at us.'[37]

Once they had arrived at Buckingham Palace, Albert asked the footman who sat at the rear of the carriage if they saw a man fire in their direction but they said they had seen nothing. Albert then ran to the balcony to see if anyone had been apprehended, but there was no commotion spotted. Since no one could corroborate the failed assassination attempt, and apparently the sound of the shot fired by Francis was not as audible as the shot fired by Edward Oxford, it was decided that the royal couple should still carry out their daily ride the next day. Victoria and Albert decided to keep the incident a secret but insisted that none of the Queen's ladies-in-waiting should accompany them on this ride in order to protect their safety.

Their caution was well placed as the following day, 30 May, Francis tried again. At 6.15 pm, as the royal couple were returning from Hampstead Heath, the would-be assassin fired a shot at Victoria on Constitution Hill, close to where Edward Oxford made a similar attempt. His pistol did not discharge and rather than make a second attempt he concealed the weapon in his coat just as a policeman standing close by seized him. Albert reported the assassination attempt in a letter to his father, Duke Ernest I of Saxe-Coburg and Gotha.

We drove out at four, giving orders to drive faster than usual, and for the two equerries, Colonel Wylde and Colonel Arbuthnot, to ride close to the carriage. You imagine that

---

37. Knight, op. cit., p.76.

The Mall, looking towards Buckingham Palace. Victoria was roughly in this area when John Francis fired a shot at her on 29 May 1842. (Author's Collection)

our minds were not very easy. We looked behind every tree, and I cast my eyes round in search of the rascal's face. We, however, got safely through the parks and drove towards Hampstead. The weather was superb, and hosts of people on foot. On our way home, as we were approaching the palace, between Green Park and the Garden Wall, a shot was fired at us at about five paces off. It was the fellow with the same pistol – a little swarthy, ill-looking rascal. The shot must have passed under the carriage, for he lowered his hand. We felt as if a load had been taken off our hearts, and we thanked the Almighty for having preserved us a second time from so great a danger.[38]

Victoria refused to be terrorised or intimidated by the second attempt upon her life and went on her usual evening drive, much to the delight of the crowds that gathered around the north-eastern entrance to Buckingham Palace on Constitution Hill. Francis was tried and

---

38. Ibid., p.78.

convicted on 17 June 1842. He was sentenced to death, although this was later commuted to transportation.

Four weeks later, John William Bean, employed as a chemist's assistant, who suffered from curvature of the spine, made another attempt to assassinate Victoria in the Mall when he fired a pistol at the Queen as she was returning from the Chapel Royal on 3 July 1842. Albert described the incident in a letter to his father.

> I have again to tell you of an attempt on Victoria's life. As we drove to the Chapel of St. James's Palace yesterday, a hunchbacked wretch tried to shoot at the carriage in which Victoria, myself and Uncle Leopold were sitting. The pistol miss fired, and a boy of sixteen (called Dassett) tore the weapon out of his hand and collard him, calling at the same time to the crowd to secure the assassin. Everybody laughed, and the people cried 'Give him back his pistol; it's only a joke.' Little Dassett and his brother, however, dragged the fellow to some policemen, who only laughed and pushed him away as making fun of them. The crowd pressed upon poor Dassett in such a way that he had to let the hunchback go. Not satisfied, however, Dassett, followed by the mob, went up to the policeman and showed him the pistol. The policeman seized him, thinking he was the culprit, and wanted to get off by shamming that he had taken the pistol from somebody else. By this time others came up who had seen the attempt, including the boy's uncle who had been present, and there was no longer any doubt of the fact. The pistol was examined by the police inspector, and was found to contain powder, paper tightly rammed down, and some pieces of clay pipe. Last night about 10 o'clock, the hunchback (whose name is Bean) was arrested.[39]

Prime Minister Sir Robert Peel immediately went to Buckingham Palace to discuss measures to protect the Queen against further attempts upon her life. In public, Peel presented a persona that was cold and self-commanding, but when he saw the Queen after this third assassination attempt he showed emotion and burst into tears. Bean was tried, convicted and imprisoned for eighteen months.

---

39. Jago, op. cit., pp.79–80.

22

Replica of Fire Fly Locomotive

Victoria's first journey by train.

On 13 June 1842, after leaving Windsor Castle, Victoria boarded a train that was driven by a Fire Fly Locomotive at Slough bound for Paddington Station, London. This was her first journey on the Great Western Railway and she became the first monarch to use the train as a means of transport. Isambard Kingdom Brunel, the renowned engineer, drove that train on the eventful journey. A replica of a Fire Fly, similar to the one used by Victoria in 1842, was built at Didcot in 2005. The Fire Fly was the first batch of a class of sixty-one locomotives used for passenger services on the Great Western Railway. Designed by Daniel Gooch and built by Jones, Turner and Evans in Newton-le-Willows, these locomotives were introduced into service in 1840 and used for thirty years until they were withdrawn in 1870.

The prospect of long-distance transport was realised in 1830 with the opening of George Stephenson's 30-mile-long Liverpool & Manchester Railway Line, which was the first inter-city railway link that relied solely upon locomotives driven by steam power. It was the first that carried passengers and the first to transport mail. The London & Birmingham Railway was completed in 1838 and trains were able to travel the 112 miles between the two cities at 20mph.

In 1833, Isambard Kingdom Brunel was appointed chief engineer on a project to construct a rail link between London and Bristol. It was a challenging task, but considerably reduced the journey time from several days to just four hours.

The Great Western Railway had been in operation for a year before it was used by Victoria. It was given two days to prepare for the Queen's first rail journey and this was done in secrecy. On 13 June 1842, Victoria made her first journey on a train from Slough Station to Paddington Station, London. The royal train consisted of the Phlegethon engine and tender drawing the royal saloon in the centre of two royal saloon carriages, preceded by a second-class carriage, and followed by three carriage trucks'.[40] Great Western Railway made efforts to decorate the royal carriages. *The Times* reported that the royal saloon, 'the fittings of which are upon a most

---

40. *Dublin Evening Post*, 16 June 1842.

A replica of a Fire Fly locomotive, which was used to pull Victoria's carriage on her first train journey on 13 June 1842. (Courtesy of Tony Hisget)

elegant and magnificent scale, were tastefully improved by bouquets of rare flowers arranged within the carriage'.[41]

The Queen arrived at Slough Station at midday and was received by Mr Russell, Chairman of the Great Western Railway, who had brought the special carriage to convey the monarch on her journey from Paddington. A crimson carpet was placed across the platform next to the reception room where the Queen waited for the train. She showed an interest in the journey, asking questions about the speed of the engine and the railways in general. Victoria was concerned about speed and gave specific instructions that the distance to Paddington should not be performed in less time than half an hour. The train departed from Slough at midday and, despite the Queen's request, it arrived at Paddington Station at 12.25 pm. In a letter to the Leopold, Victoria wrote: 'We arrived here yesterday morning, having come by the railroad, from Windsor, in half an hour, free from dust and crowd and heat, and I am quite charmed with it.'[42]

41. *The Times*, 14 June 1842.

42. Benson, Vol. 1, op. cit., p.404.

23

Figurehead from Her Majesties Yacht
Royal George

Victoria inherited HMY *Royal George* from her uncle, William IV, when she ascended the throne. HMY *Royal George* was only used once by Victoria, during her first visit to Scotland in August 1842.

HMY *Royal George* was launched at Deptford Dockyard in 1817 during the reign of George III and displaced 330 tons. The figurehead comprised the bust of George III wearing a laurel wreath, supported by two African slaves, and was inspired by Josiah Wedgewood's abolitionist medallion. The design of the figurehead was intended to celebrate the abolition of the slave trade on British soil during the reign of George III in 1807. However, it did not stop the trafficking of slaves until the Slavery Abolition Act was passed in 1833.

Victoria visited HMY *Royal George* for the first time in Portsmouth on 28 February 1842. Later that year, on 28 August, she boarded the vessel at Woolwich and this would be her first and only passage using this royal yacht, during her first visit to Scotland.

The figurehead of Her Majesties Yacht *Royal George*. (Author's Collection)

This engraving depicts Her Majesties Yacht *Royal George*, in the centre of the image flying the Royal Standard, conveying the Queen and Royal Consort to Edinburgh in August 1842. Shown just off the Bass Rock, *Royal George* has been joined by the ships *Trident* and *Monarch*. HMY *Royal George* is depicted in the centre of the image flying the Royal Standard. (Public Domain)

HMY *Royal George* pitched and rolled during the passage along the eastern coast of Britain, causing Victoria and her servants to feel symptoms of fatigue and weakness from sea sickness. HMY *Royal George* arrived at Edinburgh on 1 September 1842. On her return journey to Woolwich, she boarded the steam ship *Trident*, which was more comfortable and spacious, in comparison to *Royal George*. Victoria no longer used HMY *Royal George* as a royal yacht.

24

Walmer Castle

Victoria stayed at the castle for ten days during November 1842.

Construction of Walmer Castle began in 1539 on the orders of Henry VIII in order to strengthen the defences along the Kent coast to resist a potential French invasion. In 1727, Walmer Castle became the official residence of the Lord Warden of the Cinque Ports, when new apartments were built. The Duke of Wellington was appointed Lord Warden of the Cinque Ports in 1827 and used the apartments at the castle during the summer months, where he entertained family and friends. Victoria first visited Walmer Castle when she was a princess on 5 October 1835 with her uncle, King Leopold of Belgium. During the winter in 1842, there was an outbreak of scarlet fever in Brighton, so the Duke of Wellington invited Victoria and her family to stay at Walmer Castle for ten days during November 1842.

The close proximity to the sea and the seclusion of this stretch of coastline made this a suitable holiday destination for the royal family. The Duke of Wellington wrote of the impending royal visit to Walmer Castle in a letter to Prime Minister Sir Robert Peel:

Mr Dear Peel, – Arbuthnot has shown me your letter to him respecting this house. Nothing can be more convenient to me than to place it at Her Majesty's disposition at any time she pleases … I am only apprehensive that the accommodation in the Castle would scarcely be sufficient for Her Majesty, the Prince and the royal children, and such suite as must attend … It is the most delightful sea residence to be found anywhere, particularly for children. They can be out all day, on the ramparts and platforms quite dry, and the beautiful gardens and wood are enclosed and sheltered from severe gales of wind. There are good lodgings at Walmer village and on Walmer beach at no great distance from the Castle, not above half a mile.[43]

Despite Wellington's reservations, Victoria decided to stay at Walmer. It took the royal party nine hours, including two stops of duration fifteen minutes, to travel the 103-mile journey by horse-drawn carriage from Windsor through northern Kent to Walmer on 10 November 1842.

---

43. Benson, Vol. 1, op. cit., p.404.

Walmer Castle, Kent, where Victoria stayed during November 1842. (Author's Collection)

They arrived at Sandwich, where the royal family was welcomed by the Duke of Wellington. He escorted them to Walmer Castle and they arrived at 5 pm. Wellington vacated his rooms and stayed in the Swan Hotel, Dover, during the royal visit. Victoria used the room known as Pitt's Library in the keep. This room was originally spilt into two, serving as Wellington's dining room and as a bedroom. However, on the arrival of the Queen the bedroom was deemed too small, therefore the partition was removed to expand the bedroom. The alcove at the window served as her dressing room. Although the Duke held reservations as to the suitability of the castle to accommodate the royal family, Victoria found it comfortable.

Despite the infant Princess Royal falling ill and the Queen suffering from a cold, the royal party enjoyed the privacy at Walmer Castle. There was freedom to walk along the shingle beach towards Kingsdown in the south and towards Deal to the north without coming into contact with anyone. Brighton was unable to provide such privacy.

Victoria was charmed by her stay at Walmer. She enjoyed watching the numerous ships offshore, a sight she could not enjoy at Brighton. She spent longer than the ten days originally planned, remaining there for nearly a month.

25

Portrait of Victoria by the German Artist Franz Xaver Winterhalter in 1843

Painted during the fifth year of her reign, Victoria is depicted wearing an evening dress and the ribbon of the Order of the Garter around her left arm.

Winterhalter was a prominent artist who was commissioned by European royal families to paint portraits during the nineteenth century. He was recommended to Victoria by Queen Louise, wife of her uncle King Leopold, and in 1842 Winterhalter was commissioned to paint the British sovereign. He would return to England for seven weeks each year during her reign to paint portraits of the British royal family.

On 20 January 1843, the year that this portrait was painted, Edward Drummond, Private Secretary to Prime Minister Sir Robert Peel, was assassinated by Daniel McNaughton in Whitehall with a gunshot to the back. The assassin, who believed that he had shot the Prime Minister, was arrested. He initially said that he felt persecuted by the policies of the Tory party. Drummond's wound was initially thought to have been not serious, but the medical attention that he had received from doctors, who hastily extracted the bullet, is believed to have caused his death five days later. When McNaughton was acquitted on the grounds of insanity, Victoria, who by that time had experienced three assassination attempts, expressed concern that lunacy was used as an argument to exonerate individuals who have murdered or attempted to murder high-profile figures. The Queen kept close relations with her Prime Ministers from the beginning of her reign with Melbourne and she continued that tradition through meetings and letters with Sir Robert Peel, her Prime Minister in 1843. At the age of twenty-four, Victoria not only got involved with matters of state but took an interest in legislation. In a letter to Sir Robert on 12 March 1843, she wrote:

> The Law may be perfect, but how is it that whenever a case for its application arises, it proves to be of no avail? We have seen the trials of Oxford and McNaughton conducted by the ablest lawyers of the day – Lord Denman, Chief Justice Tindal, and Sir William

The portrait of Victoria by Franz Xaver Winterhalter painted in 1843. (Everett-Art/Shutterstock)

Follett, – and they allow and advise the Jury to pronounce the verdict of Not Guilty on account of insanity, – whilst everybody is morally convinced that both malefactors were perfectly conscious and aware of what they did![44]

44. Benson, Vol. 1, op. cit., p.469.

26

Figurehead from Her Majesties Yacht
Victoria and Albert

The figurehead of Victoria's yacht HMY *Victoria and Albert* comprised the royal arms on the starboard side and Prince Albert's arms on the port side, within a scroll, carved with acanthus leaves, roses, thistles and shamrocks. It adorns the north office block in Portsmouth Dockyard.

In 1842 the Government provided funds to build a new yacht for Victoria that would be more comfortable. A twin-paddle steamer, which were popular amongst affluent Victorians and European royalty, was chosen as the design. Victoria decided upon the name, HMY *Victoria and Albert*, and she was laid down in Pembroke Dock on 8 November 1842. It took twenty-three weeks to build the vessel. Launched on 25 April 1843, HMY *Victoria and Albert* was the first royal yacht to be steam powered, and it was owned and operated by the Royal Navy. Divided into five watertight compartments, she displaced 1,049 tons and her engines were of 458hp.

On 8 August 1843, Victoria inspected her new yacht at Deptford Dockyard, where she was being painted and prepared for service. She carefully scrutinised the fixtures and fittings and was impressed with the nursery. While she was aboard, there were seven artists painting the panels in the drawing room cabins, as well as a number of carvers and gilders embellishing the interior and exterior of the design of the yacht.

Lord Adolphus FitzClarence was appointed the first commanding officer of the new royal yacht. Her maiden voyage took place during August 1843, when Victoria sailed along the south-western coast of England. On 1 September HMY *Victoria and Albert* left Falmouth for France to transport the Queen to meet King Louis Philippe. During the passage across the English Channel, Victoria sat with her ladies-in-waiting in a sheltered place on deck near the paddle box.

The royal yacht would be used for state business and for pleasure, transporting her expanding family to Scotland for annual holidays. In 1853, the length of the yacht was increased from 200 to 260ft. Two years later, HMY *Victoria and Albert* was renamed *Osborne* 1854 while a second royal yacht was built, named HMY *Victoria and Albert II*, which was launched on 16 January 1855. *Osborne* continued to serve the royal family, transferring them from England to Osborne House on the Isle of Wight, until she was scrapped at Portsmouth during 1868.

The figurehead from Her Majesties Yacht *Victoria and Albert* in Portsmouth Dockyard. The coat of arms of Victoria are featured within the design of the figurehead on the left and the coat of arms of Prince Albert are on the right. (Courtesy of Matt Eyre)

27

Château d'Eu, Normandy

Victoria visited King Louis Phillippe I from 3 to 7 September 1843, being the first English sovereign to visit a French monarch since Henry VIII visited King Francis I in 1520.

Work to build Château d'Eu commenced in 1578 by Henri de Guise and Catherine de Cleves and was continued during the seventeenth century by the Grande Mademoiselle, cousin of King Louis XIV. It became the summer residence of Louis-Philippe during the nineteenth century, where he twice received Victoria.

Victoria had corresponded regularly with King Louis Phillippe and the purpose of the visit to France was so that she could make the personal acquaintance of the French king and his family. Louise, the king's daughter, was married to Victoria's uncle, King Leopold of Belgium. English Government ministers were unaware of the Queen's desire to visit the French king and only were alerted to the visit shortly before they departed. Before the visit, Victoria received advice from Viscount Melbourne advising her not to discuss politics or agree treaties during this visit.

The royal visit abroad also raised constitutional issues while she was overseas. The Duke of Wellington believed that a regency should be formed during the Queen's short visit to France. He retorted that:

> I was never let into the secret, nor did I believe the report then in circulation, till at last they sent to consult my opinion as to forming a regency during the Queen's absence. I immediately referred to the precedents as the only proper guide. I told them that George I, George II, (George III never went abroad), and George IV, had all been obliged to appoint Councils of Regency; that Henry VIII, when he met Francis I, at Ardres, was then master of Calais, as also when he met Charles V at Gravelines, so that in these instances, Calais being a part of his dominions, he hardly did more than pass his frontier – not much more than going from one country to the next. Upon this I decided that the Queen could not quit this country without an Act of regency. But she consulted the Crown lawyers, who decided that it was not necessary.[45]

---

45. Wilson, Vol. 1, op. cit., p.143.

The imposing Château d'Eu in Normandy. Victoria stayed at here on two occasions during September 1843. She also returned to Château d'Eu on 8 September 1845. (© Raimond Spekking/CC BY-SA 4.0; via Wikimedia Commons)

On 28 August 1843, Victoria and Albert embarked aboard the recently completed yacht HMY *Victoria and Albert* at Southampton to cross the English Channel to visit the French royal family at the Château d'Eu, near Le Tréport. They spent a couple of days sailing around the Isles of Wight and the Dorset and Devonshire coast before heading for France. The royal yacht arrived at Le Tréport during the evening of 2 September and the French king welcomed them in his barge and brought them ashore. Victoria was welcomed by a French band playing 'God save the Queen' and French locals with the words 'Vive la Reine Victoria! vive le Reine d'Angleterre!'. This was the first time that a British monarch set foot on French soil to meet a French sovereign since Henry VIII met King Francis I on the field of Cloth of Gold on 1520. Victoria recalled:

> The good, kind King was standing on the boat, and so impatient to get out, that it was very difficult to prevent him, and to get him to wait until the boat was close enough. He got out, and came up as quickly as possible, and embraced me warmly. It was a fine, and really affecting sight, and the emotion which it caused I shall never forget ... The King expressed again and again how delighted he was to see me.[46]

On leaving Le Tréport, the two sovereigns then went to the Château d'Eu, which was 8 miles from the coast. They went riding on 3 September. The band of the French 24th Regiment, Light Infantry, played beneath Victoria's window and then the royal party went to St Pierre en Valle on 4 September. When they returned to the Château d'Eu later that day, Victoria wrote to Leopold. 'I write to you from this dear place, where we are in the midst of this admirable and truly amiable family, and where we feel quite at home. Our reception by the dear King and Queen has been most kind and the people really gratifying.'[47]

---

46. Knight, op. cit., p.156.

47. Benson, Vol. 1, op. cit., p.490.

The arrival of Victoria at Château d'Eu, by Eugène-Louis Lami, 1843. (Public Domain)

Victoria was delighted to stay at Château d'Eu. She wrote, 'I felt as though it were a dream that I was at Eu, and that my favourite air castle for so many years was realised. But it is no dream, it is a pleasant reality … The Chateau is very pretty.'[48]

The visit did improve relations between Britain and France. While Victoria stayed at the Château d' Eu, French naval officers hosted Royal naval officers with a banquet aboard the French warship *Pluton*. The French king made Victoria aware of the French Navy's gesture towards the Royal Navy and at dinner at Château d'Eu expressed his desire for France to become closer allied to Britain and ensure that peace would continue in Europe.

At the end of her stay at the château, Victoria left 1,000 guineas, which was distributed among the servants who took care of her during her visit. Victoria left Château d'Eu on 7 September and set sail for Brighton aboard the royal yacht.

48. Lorne, op. cit., p.154.

28

Wood Foundation Piles of the Royal Suspension Chain Pier, Brighton

On 7 September 1843, Victoria disembarked from HMY *Victoria and Albert* at the Royal Suspension Chain Pier, Brighton, after her first visit to France.

During her visits to Brighton, Victoria would walk along the Chain Pier during the early years of her reign when she stayed at the Royal Pavilion and as a disembarkation point when her royal yacht berthed at Brighton. At low tide the wooden piles that supported the chain pier can be seen on Brighton Beach.

Designed by Captain Samuel Brown and built in 1823, the Royal Suspension Chain Pier was primary used as a landing point for packet ships to Dieppe, as well as a tourist attraction for day trippers where they could walk along its promenade. The pier was 1,154ft long and 13ft wide, and was a four-towered bridge that protruded from the cliff wall. The towers were made of cast iron, which were supported by clumps of Norwegian fir piles driven 10ft into the sea bed. Eight wrought iron chains suspended 50ft high on the cliff were threaded through the four towers. The wooden platform that allowed visitors to walk along the pier were held from 362 rods, which were suspended from these chains. Around 150 piles, paved with Portland stone, formed the T-shaped pier head. This feat of engineering became a tourist attraction as visitors marvelled at its structure that protruded into the sea. It was the first pier to be built in Brighton and could be entered by toll booth after paying a fee. The pier made Brighton a major cross-Channel ferry terminal, with several ships departing each day. However, this function was restricted during foul weather and ships would be diverted to the sheltered port at Newhaven. When a train line was established at Newhaven in 1847, Brighton's use as a continental ferry terminal fell into decline. The pier featured in paintings by Turner and Constable. In its heyday, the pier received 4,000 visitors each day, but when the West Pier was built in 1866, its novelties and entertainment attracted visitors away from the Chain Pier. The pier became obsolete and neglected, and it was destroyed by a storm on 4 December 1896. All that remains of the Chain Pier are these wooden piles.

The remains of the wood foundation piles of the Royal Suspension Chain Pier at Brighton. (Courtesy of Dominic Alves)

Victoria regarded the Chain Pier as 'a very pretty thing' when she visited Brighton during October 1837. She used it as a disembarkation point on her return passage from her visit to King Louis Phillippe on 7 September 1843. They were welcomed by a flotilla of boats, locals from Brighton and holidaymakers on the beach. Posters had been distributed across Brighton notifying the public that the Chain Pier would be closed from daybreak until the Queen had disembarked from the HMY *Victoria and Albert*. The Royal Yacht arrived at Brighton 3.30 pm.

During her final visit to Brighton, it was reported in newspapers that Victoria's private visit to the Chain Pier was the subject of public intrusion and interference. Around 9 am on 15 February 1845, Victoria and Albert left the private entrance to the Royal Pavilion in Castle Square and walked to the Chain Pier. They were dressed incognito, attired as ordinary persons to ensure they could enjoy the walk with privacy without attracting unwarranted attention. Charles Cooper, the secretary of the Chain Pier, had agreed to close the pier for two hours each morning so that the royal family could have private access. Victoria and Albert spent an hour on the Chain Pier, during which time 300 people assembled on the Marine Parade on the cliff, which overlooks the pier.

This incident did not deter the royal family from visiting the Chain Pier in the following days, except that they travelled to Marine Parade by carriage. This visit in February 1845 was Victoria's last to Brighton. She did not return and this incident probably helped her to decide to sell the Royal Pavilion and seek an alternative seaside venue where she could spend her holidays in privacy.

29

Windsor Castle

King Louis Philippe I of France was received by Victoria at Windsor Castle on 8 October 1844. This was the first visit of a French sovereign to a British monarch in peacetime.

Victoria had a strong connection with Windsor Castle. A ball was held here to celebrate her twentieth birthday in 1839. Later during that same year, in October, she proposed to Prince Albert in her private audience chamber in the castle. In February 1840 Victoria and Albert spent their three-day honeymoon at Windsor Castle. It was also the birthplace of her second son, Prince Alfred, who was born on 6 August 1844. During the early years of her reign, prior to the purchase of Osborne House, Victoria sought solace from public life at Windsor Castle. In a letter to Leopold, she wrote: 'Windsor is beautiful and comfortable, but it is a palace, and God knows how willingly I would always live with my beloved Albert and our children in the quiet and retirement of private life, and not be the constant object of observation, and of newspaper articles.'[49]

The essayist Leigh Hunt wrote that: 'Windsor Castle is a place to receive monarchs in; Buckingham Palace to fashion in; and Kensington Palace seems a place to drink tea in.'[50] Windsor Castle is the oldest occupied castle in the world and played a prominent role in receiving foreign dignitaries. Victoria used Windsor Castle to host heads of state with the purpose of improving diplomatic relations, developing commerce between nations and preserving peace, such as the state visit and King Louis Phillippe of France on 8 October 1844. When the French king arrived, she wrote: 'He is the first King of France who comes on a visit to the Sovereign of this country. A very eventful epoch, indeed, and one which will surely bring good fruits.'[51]

The French king was welcomed by the cheers of thousands of spectators who lined the Long Walk and the sounds of the bells pealing from St George's Chapel before being warmly received by Victoria and her mother, the Duchess of Kent, at the entrance. A dinner took place in the dining room at Windsor Castle during that evening.

---

49. Benson, Vol. 2, op. cit., p.5.

50. Ball, Frederick T., *Queen Victoria: Scenes and Incidents of Her Life and Reign* (A.G. Watson, Toronto, Canada, 1888), p.14.

51. Browne, Gordon, *Queen Victoria* (George G. Harrap & Company, London, 1915), p.49.

An aerial view of Windsor Castle. Prior to the state visit of King Louis Phillippe, Victoria used Windsor to host the King of Prussia in 1842 and Emperor Nicholas of Russia in 1844. (EQRoy/Shutterstock)

On the following day, Victoria and Albert walked with their French guests from the royal apartments to St George's Chapel, King Louis Phillippe expressed an interest in the two-handed sword that belonged to Edward III that hung in the chapel adjacent to his portrait. The heavy sword, which was 7ft long, was taken down and placed in the hands of the French king. Afterwards, with Victoria holding his arm, Louis Phillippe returned to the inner precincts of Windsor Castle, near St George's Gate, from where they walked down the Home Park to the dairy that was established by Prince Albert. Here the Prince Consort had created a business that produced dairy products that was commercially successful. A state banquet was held during that evening in St George's Hall.

On 10 October, King Louis Phillippe visited Claremont and Hampton Court Palace, Claremont and Twickenham, where he had the opportunity to visit places where he lived during exile. On returning later that evening to Windsor Castle, the Queen hosted dinner in St George's Hall. During the following day he toured Woolwich Arsenal and visited Eton College. During that evening Victoria installed the French king as a Knight of the Garter.

The state visit ended on 14 October 1844 when King Louis Philippe left Windsor Castle and began his journey home. The French king enjoyed his stay at Windsor Castle. He assured the Queen that France did not want to go to war with Britain and the visit helped to resolve differences.

30

Osborne House

Victoria and Albert purchased the Osborne Estate on the Isle of Wight during May 1845.

Victoria owned three homes at Windsor Castle, Buckingham Palace and the Royal Pavilion at Brighton. Although they were ideal for carrying out state ceremonial functions, they were not fit for raising a growing family. Buckingham Palace had gardens, but the nurseries were in the attic. Windsor Castle had nurseries for the children and rooms for their nurses, but no gardens. The Royal Pavilion was situated in the centre of Brighton and was not conducive to their desire for privacy, so they looked for a suitable property.

Victoria and Albert sought a place of privacy in the country. She favoured the Isle of Wight as a place to live, having stayed there during her childhood. Prime Minister Sir Robert Peel, recommended Osborne House, which was a mile east of Cowes. On 15 October 1844, Victoria visited Osborne for the first time and was enchanted by the place. She wrote: 'It is a very comfortable little house, and the grounds and place are delightful, so private – and the view so fine.'[52]

Osborne offered the royal family walks in the country that could be walked in total privacy. Being close to the sea, they had a private beach and facilities where they could land boats. In May 1845 Victoria and Albert purchased the Osborne estate, including the old house, for £26,000 (value in 2017, £2 million) at their own expense, which meant that it was a private royal residence. Victoria wrote to Melbourne:

> We were so occupied and delighted with our new and really delightful home … It is impossible to imagine a prettier spot – valleys and woods which would be beautiful anywhere; but all this near the sea (the woods grow into the sea) is quite perfection. We have a charming beach quite to ourselves. The sea was so blue and calm that the Prince said it was like Naples. And then we can walk about anywhere by ourselves without being followed and mobbed, which Lord Melbourne will easily understand is delightful. And last, not least, we have Portsmouth and Spithead so close at hand, that we shall be able to watch what is going on, which will please the Navy, and be hereafter very useful for our boys.[53]

52. Benson, Vol. 2, op. cit., p.26.

53. Ibid., p.36.

A view of Osborne House. (Courtesy of Paul Farmer; www.geograph.org.uk)

The house was too small, so it was decided to build a new house to suit their needs and then demolish the old one. Osborne House was designed by builder Thomas Cubitt in an Italian style, featuring high towers. The first stone of the Pavilion wing was laid by Victoria and Albert on 23 June 1845. Building was completed within a year and they were able to reside in this wing during 1846. Work continued to build the two eastern wings, to accommodate guests and the royal household, from 1845 to 1851. During the following fifty years, Victoria and the royal family could enjoy a quiet life by the seaside, where they spent pleasurable days on the private beach. Victoria's first experience of bathing in the sea and using a bathing machine took place on 30 July 1847 at her private beach within the Osborne estate.

The bathing machine on display at Osborne Beach consists of a changing room and a toilet. It stands on the original stone rails that were used to lower the bathing machine into the sea. The royal children were taught to swim at Osborne Beach. Albert created an enclosed area for them to learn safely using two pontoons. He would take the older princes for daily swims. Eugene Loby, a young French woman from Boulogne, came to Osborne to teach the younger princesses to swim.

Albert could devote time to his scientific interests at Osborne and was the driving force in installing innovations to the house, including a ventilation system and hot showers, He was also responsible for the construction of the Swiss chalet, which he used as a classroom to teach

This bathing machine was used by Victoria and her family when they went swimming on Osborne Beach. After Victoria's death, the bathing machine was used as a chicken shed, before it was relocated to its current position in 1927. (Courtesy of Paul Farmer; www.geograph.org.uk)

his children. Osborne House was a happy environment to raise a family. After the death of Albert in 1861, Osborne House became a place of solace where Victoria could grieve in private solitude, and it became her preferred place of residence.

Although Osborne House provided a refuge to escape from ceremonies of state, the calm and peaceful environment gave Victoria the opportunity to concentrate on matters of state and she would often receive Prime Ministers, heads of state and royal dignitaries from abroad there, including Emperor Napoleon III and Kaiser Wilhelm II. During 1882 she received Cetshwayo, the King of Zululand.

It was at Osborne House on 14 January 1878, that Alexander Graham Bell, the American inventor, gave Victoria a demonstration in the use of the telephone. Bell was with the Queen in the Council Room and they were able to use the telephone to speak to Sir Thomas and Mary Biddolph, who were at Osborne Cottage. At the same time, he made the first publicly witnessed long-distance calls from Osborne House to Cowes, Southampton and London. Victoria was impressed and asked if she could purchase a telephone.[54]

Victoria died at Osborne House on 22 January 1901. After her death, Edward VII presented it to the nation. It became a Naval Training College and is now a tourist attraction administered by English Heritage.

---

54. Buckle, George Earle, *The Letters of Queen Victoria, A selection of from Her Majesty's correspondence between the years 1862 and 1878, Volume 2* (Published John Murray, London 1926), p.594.

31

SS *Great Britain*

Victoria inspected Brunel's steam passenger ship at Blackwall, London, on 22 April 1845.

SS *Great Britain* was built specifically for the Great Western Steamships Company's Bristol to New York service and would hold the record for being the longest passenger ship for nine years, between 1845 and 1854. Designed by Isambard Kingdom Brunel, it was the first ocean-going vessel to be constructed of iron and feature a screw propeller. Launched in Bristol in the presence of Prince Albert on 19 July 1843, it took a further two years to complete. Once it was built, *Great Britain* was brought to Blackwell for inspection by Victoria.

Victoria boarded the royal steam tender named *Dwarf* at Greenwich on 22 April 1845, cheered by Greenwich Pensioners as she was conveyed eastwards along the River Thames towards Blackwell, where *Great Britain* was moored. *Lloyd's Weekly Newspaper* reported that: 'Her Majesty wore a tartan silk dress, and Paisley shawl with a bright blue bonnet and appeared in the enjoyment of excellent health.'[55]

Once aboard, the royal standard was hoisted on the mainmast of *Great Britain*. Victoria then received a guided tour of the vessel from Isambard Kingdom Brunel, who explained how the screw propeller propelled the vessel. Before disembarking from *Great Britain*, the Queen addressed its commander, Captain Hosken, and said: 'I am very much gratified with the sight of your magnificent ship, and I wish you every possible success on your voyages across the Atlantic.'[56]

The maiden voyage of *Great Britain* began from Liverpool on 26 July 1845 with forty-five passengers. The passage between Liverpool and New York took fourteen days and twenty-one hours. The return passage took thirteen days, twelve hours. *Great Britain* was the largest and fastest passenger liner of its day. In 1852, it made its maiden voyage from Britain to Melbourne, transporting migrants to Australia who were about to embark on their search for gold. The passenger liner would continue sailing this route for a further thirty years, briefly interrupted in 1855 when she was requisitioned as a troopship during the Crimean War. On 8 August 1855,

---

55. *Lloyd's Weekly Newspaper*, 27 April 1845.

56. Ibid.

SS *Great Britain* at Bristol.
(Electric Egg/Shutterstock)

Victoria welcomed *Great Britain* when she arrived at Spithead with wounded soldiers from the Crimea. She wrote:

> In the afternoon, we went on board the *'Fairy'* & steamed up to Spithead, to look at the *'Great Britain'*, arrived this morning with 174 invalids & 13 Officers. They crowded the deck as we passed, all cheering loudly. It is an immense ship, which Albert went to see launched at Bristol, 11 or 12 years ago. The sea was quite rough.[57]

Great Britain was also used as a troopship during the Indian Mutiny during 1857. Her role as a passenger liner came to an end during April 1886 when she sustained several leaks and lost two masts while passing round Cape Horn. She was brought to Port Stanley, Falkland Islands, where it was learnt that it was too expensive to repair her. *Great Britain* was sold to the Falkland Island Company, who used it as a store ship for wood and coal. In 1937 *Great Britain* was beached at Sparrow Cove, where she was abandoned until 24 April 1971, She then began her final journey to Bristol, where she is on display as a museum.

---

57. Royal Archives: RA VIC/MAIN/QVJ (W), 8 August 1855 (Courtesy HM Queen Elizabeth II).

32

Cambridge House

Robert Pate assaulted Victoria with a walking cane outside Cambridge House, Piccadilly, on 27 June 1850.

Victoria made numerous visits to her uncle, the Duke of Cambridge, who was seriously ill at his London residence. On 27 June 1850, she visited him with her children, the Prince of Wales, Prince Alfred and Princess Alice, accompanied by her lady-in-waiting, Viscountess Jocelyn, escorted by equerry, Colonel, the Honourable, Charles Grey on horseback. After leaving Cambridge House in an open carriage, Victoria, who was sad and solemn as a result of her uncle's ill health, was struck across the face with a cane as her carriage turned into Piccadilly. The assault was carried out by a respectably dressed man, who maintained the appearance of a gentleman. Robert Renwick, the Queen's Sergeant Footman, who was seated behind the Queen in the carriage, seized the assailant after he struck Her Majesty and held him until he was dragged away by a disgruntled mob, one of which struck Pate in retaliation. Pate was arrested by Sergeant Silver of C Division, who took him to Vine Street Police Station.

The bonnet that Victoria was wearing provided some protection, however she received some bruising to her face and forehead. Her physician, Sir James Clark, reported that: 'I examined her Majesty's forehead and found a considerable tumour on the outer angle of the right brow, and a small cut. It had been bleeding, but the blood had stopped. I was surprised to see so much injury done by such a small stick, and I therefore infer it was used very violently. Her Majesty's bonnet was cut through. I think the skin was cut by the stick, and not by the wire margin of the bonnet.'[58]

Robert Pate, aged forty-three, a former lieutenant who had served with the 10th Hussars in the British Army for four years, was identified as the culprit. He had used 'a small partridge cane, about two feet, two inches long, with a curved hook for a handle and a small brass ferule at the end'.[59]

Undeterred by the violent ordeal, Victoria proceeded to Buckingham Palace, where she received her Prime Minister, Lord John Russell at 9 pm. Twenty minutes later she continued with her plans to visit the Royal Italian Opera (now known as the Royal Opera House) at Covent Garden with the Prince of Prussia, where they watched an Italian opera.

---

58. *Morning Chronicle*, 12 July 1850.

59. *Globe*, 29 June 1850.

Above: Cambridge House in Piccadilly. (Courtesy of Julian Osley; www.geograph.org.uk)

Right: An illustration depicting Robert Pale's attack upon Victoria outside Cambridge House. (Author's Collection)

Robert Pate was tried on 12 July 1850 at the Central Criminal Court, the Old Bailey, where no motive was ascertained and the jury refused to accept his plea of insanity. Pate was found guilty of assaulting the Queen and sentenced to seven years' transportation to Tasmania.

33

Marble Arch

Marble Arch was relocated from the entrance to Buckingham Palace to Hyde Park Corner in 1851.

In 1828 George IV commissioned John Nash as architect to design a triumphal arch that would celebrate the victories during the Napoleonic wars at Trafalgar and Waterloo, and he intended to surmount the structure with an equestrian statue of his patron. Nash's design was inspired by the Arch of Constantine in Rome and was built using white Carrara marble. By 1830, the panels and statues designed by Nash that were to adorn the arch had been built. The plan to erect an equestrian statue of George IV was abandoned when he died and the Duke of Wellington dismissed Nash from the project because he had overspent. Edward Blore was commissioned to complete the project at a lower cost.

Nash was angry that he was dismissed and refused to co-operate in revealing how he had intended to use the panels and statues, so Blore had to decipher the plan like a jigsaw puzzle. The battle friezes were incorporated in the central courtyard of Buckingham Palace. Some of the sculptures were given to William Wilkins, who was working on the construction of the National Gallery. The equestrian statue of George IV was positioned on a plinth in the north-eastern corner of Trafalgar Square.

The arch was completed in 1833 and gates were installed during 1837. Victoria passed through the arch on the day of her coronation in 1838 and it served as the main entrance to Buckingham Palace for seventeen years.

When Edward Blore was commissioned to renovate and expand Buckingham Palace to accommodate the increasing royal family, he built an east wing that enclosed the courtyard and this meant that Marble Arch was no longer required. In 1850, a decision was made to relocate it from Buckingham Palace to Cumberland Gate, at the north-eastern corner of Hyde Park and the western entrance to Oxford Street. Thomas Cubitt oversaw the operation to transfer the arch, which took three months and was completed during March 1851. Horses and wagons transported the blocks of marble from the palace to the new location. Builders worked through the night under gaslight to get the work completed. A police station was constructed in an upper chamber of Marble Arch where a reserve of policemen could be based.

In 1851, Marble Arch formed a magnificent entrance into the Great Exhibition, which took place in Hyde Park. From there visitors would get their first glimpse of the majestic Crystal

Right: A view of the southern face of Marble Arch. (Author's Collection)

Below: Entitled *The New Palace*, this painting by James Arthur O'Connor features Marble Arch at the entrance, which would have been familiar to Victoria when she ascended the throne. (Anne S.K. Brown Military Collection, Brown University Library)

Palace. Marble Arch remained the primary entrance into the park for the following fifty years but during the twentieth century it became isolated on an island surrounded by roads.

Only members of the royal family and the King's Troop, Royal Horse Artillery, are permitted to pass through Marble Arch.

34

Crystal Palace

Victoria attended the opening of the Great Exhibition at Crystal Palace in Hyde Park, London, on 1 May 1851.

The notion of the Great Exhibition was conceived when Henry Cole and a delegation from the Society of Arts visited an exhibition in Paris in 1844 that promoted products of French industry. Cole proposed a similar exhibition to promote British industry and its achievement and needed support from a Royal Commission.

In January 1850, Prince Albert was appointed Chairman of that commission and began the planning of the Great Exhibition. Former Prime Ministers Lord John Russell and Sir Robert Peel belonged to the committee alongside architects Charles Barry and Thomas Cubitt. The Great Exhibition was not a public event because Parliament did not support the initiative, which meant that Albert had to raise funds of £200,000 (£16 million in 2017) from the private sector in the City of London. In a speech to city financiers at Mansion House in March 1850, he spoke of the objectives of the exhibition and sought financial support. Albert wanted to use the Great Exhibition as a vehicle to assess achievements in technology and to unify nations.

Construction of Crystal Palace began on 30 July 1850 on ground between Albert Gate and Knightsbridge Barracks on the east and west, and between Rotten Row and St George's Place on south and north. Two thousand men were employed on the project and they worked day and night.

Crystal Palace became the largest enclosed space during that time, measuring 563m long and 124m wide. It encompassed 26 acres and 300,000 panes of glass were used in its construction. The space could accommodate 13,000 exhibitors, with 100,000 exhibits, which were mainly British. Crystal Palace epitomised Albert's vision of displaying the best that Britain could offer the world as a nation.

On 29 April 1851, two days before the official opening, Victoria paid a private visit to Crystal Palace. She returned two days later on 1 May to open the Great Exhibition. When she arrived, there was an estimated 250,000 spectators lining the route and 700,000 people in Green Park and Hyde Park who had congregated to watch the Queen, accompanied by her children, Vicky and Bertie, in a procession of nine state carriages escorted by the Life Guards.

The impressive Crystal Palace in Hyde Park. (Courtesy of the British Library)

An estimated 40,000 people visited the Great Exhibition on its opening day. Victoria was entranced by the splendour of Crystal Palace, fascinated by the exhibition and proud that this major event was accomplished by her husband.

The exhibition was divided into four sections, Raw materials, Machinery, Manufactures and Sculpture and the fine arts. The first public conveniences with flushing toilets appeared at the Great Exhibition and heralded the first public lavatories, known as 'waiting rooms', which were opened in Britain the following year.

The Great Exhibition closed on 15 October 1851 and was considered a tremendous success, attracting 6 million visitors during the six months that it was open. On its final day, 55,000 visitors came to Crystal Palace. It was not only enjoyed by local Londoners, but special trains brought visitors from the northern industrial cities to London so that they could visit the exhibition and marvel at the grandeur of Crystal Palace. Those who lived in London were so impressed with what they saw that they returned many times to visit the exhibition. Victoria spent only an hour at Crystal Palace on the opening day, but she returned to the exhibition on numerous occasions to spend time looking at specific galleries.

35

Memorial to the Great Exhibition Outside the Royal Albert Hall

Tourists flock to see the impressive Albert Memorial that stands north of the Royal Albert Hall, but to the south of this iconic building there exists the Memorial to the Great Exhibition, which features the Prince Consort who organised the event.

The Great Exhibition was Prince Albert's greatest achievement; the passion, labour and dedication to the creation of this spectacular event consumed all his energy at the time. Victoria wrote:

The triumph is immense, for up to the last hour the difficulties, the opposition, and the ill-natured attempts to annoy and frighten, of a certain set of fashionables and Protectionists, were immense, but Albert's temper, patience, firmness and energy surmounted all, and the feeling is universal.[60]

Although it did not secure peace around the world, the exhibition was considered a commercial success and earned a profit of £250,000 (£20 million in 2017), which was used to invest in the establishment of museums in South Kensington. Albert's organisation of the Great Exhibition together with Victoria's support and patronage had aligned the royal family with its success and with the success of Britain's strength as an affluent, industrialised, commercial nation, at the same time increasing the popularity of the royal family.

In 1853 it was decided to commemorate the Great Exhibition using surplus profits that the exhibition had generated. Artists were invited to propose ideas and designs for a memorial to celebrate the event. Fifty artists submitted their proposals and Joseph Durham's idea was chosen. He envisaged an image of Britannia standing above a plinth and four representations of the four corners of the world. Finding a suitable location close to Hyde Park to install the monument proved problematic, but the Royal Horticultural Society provided space in their grounds at the south side of the park. Prince Albert unveiled the memorial in 1861, but after he died later that year it was decided to replace the statue of Britannia with a sculpture of the late Prince Consort, in recognition of the important part he played in the organisation of the Great

---

60. Benson, Vol. 2, op. cit., pp.317–8.

Exhibition. The redesigned monument was inaugurated by the Prince and Princess of Wales in 1863. During the redevelopment and transformation of Kensington as a centre of museums and learning, the monument was transferred to its current location, south of the Royal Albert Hall and overlooking Prince Consort Road.

The memorial is 40ft high and is constructed using red and grey granite and Portland stone. The figures of Prince Albert and the four sculptures signifying the four corners of the globe are made of bronze. Bronze copies of medals awarded to the Exhibition adorn the plinth. The biblical quotation is inscribed on the memorial 'Let the nations be gathered together and the people be assembled', reflecting the international appeal of the Great Exhibition that included exhibits that showcased global innovative advances in technology and the arts, as well as attracting people from around the world to visit it.

The memorial to the Great Exhibition in front of the Albert Hall. (Author's Collection)

36

The Sovereign's Entrance, Victoria Tower, Palace of Westminster

Victoria entered the Houses of Parliament through the newly built Sovereign's Entrance for the State Opening of Parliament on 3 February 1852.

After the destruction of the Palace of Westminster by fire in 1834, plans were established in 1835 to consider rebuilding the palace. The design was decided by a competition from which the commission received ninety-seven proposals, each identified by a pseudonym or a symbol. The architect Charles Barry was the successful architect and his proposal was numbered sixty-four, adorned by the emblem of the portcullis. Barry decided not to use the old plan of the original palace but to adopt a Gothic style, which would also preserve and incorporate the surviving Westminster Hall, the Undercroft Chapel and the Cloisters of St Stephen's Chapel.

Before work could begin, the ruins of the existing palace had to be demolished, sewers had to be diverted and 8 acres of land had to be reclaimed from the River Thames. Construction began in 1840, but it would take approximately thirty years to complete and cost more than £2 million (£160 million in 2017), despite Barry estimating it would take just six years to build at a cost of £724,986 (£58 million). In 1841, Prince Albert chaired a Royal Commission to decide upon the interior design of the palace in October 1841.

While the new palace was being constructed the House of Lords used the Painted Chamber and the House of Commons sat in the Lesser Hall, which were hastily restored to accommodate the two houses. The House of Lords was able to use the specially built chamber in 1847 and the House of Commons was able to occupy the new chamber in 1852.

Barry incorporated the cypher VR, *Victoria Regina*, of the reigning monarch throughout the Palace of Westminster together with the Tudor Rose and portcullis. The tallest tower of the Palace of Westminster, in the north-western corner of the estate, was initially named the King's Tower. It was renamed Victoria's Tower in 1897 in honour of the Queen during her Diamond anniversary year. The tower situated at the north-eastern corner that holds the Great Bell, commonly known as Big Ben, was named the Elizabeth Tower after the Tudor queen.

Victoria's Tower contains twelve floors and its primary purpose was to act as a fireproof repository for books and documents from the parliamentary archives. It was also designed specifically as an entrance for the monarch to enter the Palace of Westminster and for many

Victoria entered the Palace of Westminster through the Sovereign's Entrance on 3 February 1852. (Ivica Drusany/Shutterstock)

years it was regarded as the tallest stone square tower in the world measuring, 375ft. The tower is surmounted by an iron flagpole from which the Union Jack is flown, and when the sovereign is present inside the building the Royal Standard is raised. Opulent statues of the patron saints of England, Scotland, Ireland and Wales, together with a statue of Victoria and two symbolic figures representing Justice and Mercy, decorate the interior of the gateway of the Sovereign's Entrance, which was built sufficiently wide enough to allow Victoria's Gold State Coach to enter the Palace of Westminster.

On 3 February 1852, Victoria arrived at the newly built Houses of Parliament in this coach, entering the Victoria Tower, now known as the Sovereign's Entrance for the first State Opening of Parliament at the newly built Palace of Westminster. Charles Barry welcomed Victoria as she entered the Sovereign's entrance. She was so impressed with the design of the entrance that she wrote to Prime Minister Lord John Russell, 'the Houses of Lords and Commons being now almost completed, and the Queen having entered the House of Lords by the Grand Entrance (which is magnificent), the Queen thinks this will be the right moment of bestowing on Mr Barry the knighthood, as a mark of the Queen's approbation of his great work'.[61]

Barry was knighted by Victoria in that same year and although most of the building was completed by 1860, it would take a further decade for it to be totally finished. Barry would not live to see the finished building because he died in 1860.

---

61. Benson, Vol. 2, op. cit., p.363.

37

The Sovereign's Throne,
House of Lords

The first State Opening of Parliament conducted by Victoria in the rebuilt House of Lords within the Palace of Westminster took place on 3 February 1852 and it was from the Sovereign's Throne that she delivered the Queen's Speech.

Victoria's first visit to the Houses of Parliament was on 17 July 1837 when she had to dissolve Parliament before the general election that was triggered by the death of William IV. Victoria was the last monarch to dissolve Parliament for this reason because the immediate dissolution of Parliament following the demise of the monarch was abolished by the Reform Act in 1867. It was during her first visit that she addressed both the House of Commons and Lords from the House of Lords.

Victoria returned to the House of Lords on 20 November 1837 for the first State Opening of Parliament, which is carried out at the start of the parliamentary year, or after a general election. The ceremony, permeated in pomp and pageantry, shows the sovereign's relationship between Crown and Parliament and his or her role in the constitution. Victoria read the Queen's Speech to the House of Lords and Members of Parliament, who were summoned to listen from the House of Commons. The ceremony marks the beginning of the Parliamentary session. The sovereign comes to the House of Lords to deliver the Queen's Speech, which is written by the Government of the day and sets out its agenda, policies and future legislation. It is the only occasion where the sovereign, the House of Lords and Members of Parliament from the House of Commons officially meet.

Victoria regularly attended the State Opening of Parliament each year during the first twenty-four years of her reign. In 1852, it took place on 3 February 1852 and it was the first time that Victoria read the Queen's Speech in the newly built Houses of Parliament and from the Sovereign's Throne. The chair was designed by A.W.N. Pugin in 1847 and it was constructed by John Webb of Bond Street. Pugin's design was influenced by the design of St Edward's Chair, known as the Coronation Chair, in which Victoria was crowned in Westminster Abbey. The Sovereign's Throne is made of wood, carved and gilded with rock crystals and upholstered in red velvet and intricate embroidery.

After the death of Albert in 1861, the Queen participated in the state ceremony less frequently. She was persuaded by Lord John Russell to return to the House of Lords in 1866 to open Parliament from the Sovereign's Throne, the first time since the death of her husband.

The Sovereign's Throne in the House of Lords. (Courtesy of Photographer/House of Lords)

Changes were made to the ceremony to reflect her sombre mood; firstly there was silence, instead of the usual flourish of trumpets as she entered Parliament. Instead of her wearing the robe of state, this garment was draped across the Sovereign's Throne and the Queen's Speech was read by the Lord Chancellor instead of being delivered by the Queen.

38

Snow-Type Chloroform Inhaler

At 1.10 am on 7 April 1853, Victoria became the first notable person to test out a new drug called chloroform during the birth of her eighth child, Leopold. Doctor John Snow administered the drug, which alleviated the labour pains that she was suffering during childbirth. Here is an example of an inhaler designed by Snow of a type that Victoria would have used to take the anaesthetic.

Childbirth during the nineteenth century was extremely risky if there were complications, putting the lives of the mother and baby in jeopardy. It was highly dangerous; however, Victoria would bear nine children successfully. The experience of pregnancy and childbirth caused Victoria physical discomfort and suffering, which was extremely traumatic.

Victoria detested the pain endured during labour and being confined to her room, unable to perform her duties as sovereign during these times. Doctor John Snow was a renowned physician regarded as the leading pioneer in the field of anaesthetics in Britain. He learned of anaesthetics being used in the United States in 1846. Snow conducted tests on the effects of chloroform, a colourless, sweet-smelling liquid on animals to ensure that it could be safely administered to people so they could be dazed or knocked out during operations or when suffering pain. In 1847 Snow devised an inhaler that could be used to administer chloroform. One canister was used for chloroform and the other for cold water, which would connect to the brass facemask, lined with velvet by a flexible tube, to enable the patient to inhale the anaesthetic vapours.

Chloroform was used as an anaesthetic to transform childbirth and offer women pain relief. Victoria had heard about its use and was keen to try it during the birth of her sixth child in 1848, but Doctor Charles Locock, her obstetrician advised against it. However, during her eighth pregnancy, with the support of Albert, she decided to use it. Remarkably, she had to seek permission from the Archbishop of Canterbury. Doctor John Snow was summoned to Buckingham Palace on 7 April 1853 to administer the anaesthetic during the birth of Prince Leopold. Victoria recorded in her journal, 'that blessed Chloroform … the effect was soothing, quieting and delightful beyond measure'.[62] The application of chloroform enabled Victoria to recover from the childbirth more quickly as a consequence of her suffering being alleviated.

---

62. Royal Archives: RA VIC/MAIN/QVJ (W), 22 April 1853 (Courtesy HM Queen Elizabeth II).

An example of a snow-type chloroform inhaler, circa 1848–70. (Science Museum, London/Wellcome Collection)

Chloroform had been available since 1847, but Victoria's use of the anaesthesia endorsed Doctor Snow's method and encouraged other women to try this method of pain relief during childbirth. Four years later, Doctor Snow would administer chloroform to Victoria during the birth of her ninth child, Princess Beatrice, on 14 April 1857.

Victoria would later use chloroform on 1 August 1867 at Osborne House when she was suffering from toothache, which necessitated an extraction. When an abscess appeared on her arm and had to be removed, she used chloroform again on 4 September 1871. She wrote:

I felt dreadfully nervous, as I bear pain so badly. I shall be given chloroform, but not very much, as I am so far from well otherwise, so I begged the part might be frozen which was agreed on. – Everything was got ready and the three doctors came in. Sir William Jenner gave me some whiffs of chloroform, whilst Mr Lister froze the place, Dr Marshall holding my arm. The abscess, which was 6 inches in diameter, was very quickly cut & I hardly felt anything excepting the last touch, when I was given a little more chloroform. In an instant there was relief. I was then tightly bandaged, & rested on my bed.[63]

63. Royal Archives: RA VIC/MAIN/QVJ (W), 4 September 1871 (Courtesy HM Queen Elizabeth II).

39

The Balcony, Buckingham Palace

Victoria watched from the balcony as the First Battalion, Scots Fusilier Guards, departed for the Crimean War on 28 February 1854.

The central balcony on the eastern façade of Buckingham Palace was incorporated within Edward Blore's design for the eastern wing in 1846. From this balcony Victoria watched the Guards that paraded at Horse Guards Parade for her birthday return to Buckingham Palace on 27 May 1847. This set a precedent for future birthdays and the annual Trooping of the Colour ceremony.

The use of this balcony as the focal point for national celebration where the sovereign celebrated with her people began on 1 May 1851, when Victoria stood on the balcony and was warmly received after she had opened the Great Exhibition in Hyde Park. The British Army received orders to deploy to the Crimea on 20 February 1854. On 28 February, Victoria and her family stood on the balcony at Buckingham Palace and saw the last contingent of Guards, the First Battalion, Scots Fusilier Guards, depart. It was her express wish that the battalion pass in full marching order before Buckingham Palace so that her family and the public could support them on their departure for the impending war. The battalion was mustered before its commander, Colonel Dixon, at 6 am at Wellington Barracks, before marching to Waterloo Station via Buckingham Palace. At 7 am they paraded at the palace before Victoria, who was standing on the balcony. The First Battalion, being formed in line, presented arms and gave three cheers for Her Majesty. The *London Evening Standard* described the scene as the battalion marched into the palace courtyard from Birdcage Walk:

> On the battalion arriving at Buckingham Palace, and entering the south gate, her Majesty, his Royal Highness Prince Albert, his Royal Highness the Prince of Wales, the Princess Royal and Princess Helena appeared on the balcony in front of the Palace. When the whole of the men had marched into the enclosure, they formed in line and presented arms, the band played 'God save the Queen' [...] her Majesty frequently bowing to the cheering of the vast crowd assembled. The order to recover arms was then given, and the entire battalion simultaneously took off their bearskin caps and gave three hearty cheers.

The balcony at Buckingham Palace. Victoria set the tradition for appearing on the balcony during times of national celebration after opening the Great Exhibition on 1 May 1851. (Author's Collection)

> Her Majesty seemed much struck with the novelty of such enthusiasm on the part of so splendid a body of men about to proceed to the seat of war and frequently expressed her acknowledgement.[64]

Two years later, Victoria welcomed approximately 3,200 soldiers belonging to the Grenadier, Coldstream and Scots Fusilier Guards from the same balcony at Buckingham Palace when they returned from the Crimean War at midday on 9 July 1856. They marched from the Mall and entered the South Gate into the Buckingham Palace and beneath the balcony. On this occasion, her uncle, King Leopold of Belgium, stood on the balcony as Victoria welcomed home her soldiers.

The First Battalion, Scots Fusilier Guards, numbered 880 men when two years previously they saluted Victoria as she bade them farewell. When they returned to march past the Queen at Buckingham Palace only 304 remained.

The balcony was decorated with red cloth and it is a tradition that has continued since that day when the Royal family appear upon it for royal weddings, Trooping of the Colour and

---

64. *London Evening Standard*, 28 February 1854.

This engraving by Augustus Butler and Charles William Glover depicts troops parading past Buckingham Palace on 9 July 1856, following their return from the Crimean War. Victoria can be seen on the balcony. (Anne S.K. Brown Military Collection, Brown University Library)

other special occasions. Victoria was elated by the appearance of her soldiers as they paraded before her. She wrote: 'I felt as if I were doing so little and would have liked to grasp their hands and greet them!'[65]

The balcony would become pivotal in the relationship between the sovereign and her people. It was where she could be seen and engage with her subjects, and it would be the focal point of all royal and national events.

---

65. Royal Archives: RA VIC/MAIN/QVJ (W), 9 July 1856 (Courtesy HM Queen Elizabeth II).

40

Military Jacket Worn by Victoria

Being sovereign meant that Victoria was Head of the Armed Forces and therefore required a military uniform. Although she never knew her father, she was always proud that she was the daughter of a soldier. The design of the tunic in this painting emulated the masculine uniform, but it is feminised with an allayed shoulder line and embellished waist. This military jacket was worn by Victoria when inspecting her soldiers on their return from the Crimean War.

Victoria was eager to play an active role to support the war effort, so with her daughters and the ladies of her household she knitted woollen socks and mittens for the troops fighting on the peninsular. Although she was unable to visit the Crimea, she took her role as Head of the Armed Forces seriously and when war appeared imminent towards the end of the summer of 1853, she was reluctant to leave London for her holiday in Scotland. Lord Aberdeen, the Prime Minister, had assured her that she would be consulted on crucial decisions regarding conflict and the deployment of her forces. While at Balmoral Castle in Scotland, Victoria was furious to learn that Lord Palmerston, Home Secretary, had encouraged Lord Aberdeen to deploy the Royal Navy and Army to the Black Sea in anticipation of war without her consent. In a letter to Leopold, Victoria showed that she was concerned how the war would eventually develop, the inadequacies of the British Army as a fighting force and the security of home shores: 'But we are going to make war against Russia! …We engage in a war which may assume in its course a totally different corner from that of its beginning. Who can say that our own shores may be threatened by powers now in alliance with us? We are powerless for offence or defence without a trained Army. To obtain this will require considerable time.'[66]

Splits within the British Government were caused by the Reform Bill and Victoria advised Secretary of State for the Colonies, Lord John Russell, of the importance for the members of the Cabinet to present a united front as the nation was about to go to war. 'The Queen seizes this opportunity of expressing her sense of the imperative importance of the Cabinet being united and of one mind at this moment, and not to let it appear that there are differences of opinion within it. The knowledge that there are such is a cause of GREAT anxiety to the Queen, at a time when she is to enter a European War, of which nobody can confidently predict the extent.'[67]

---

66. Benson, Vol. 3, op. cit., p.12.

67. Ibid., p.15.

Accompanied by Prince Albert and other officers, Victoria, mounted in semi-military costume, observes a military exercise in the valley below, Aldershot, 1858. (Anne S.K. Brown Military Collection, Brown University Library)

Victoria read daily dispatches from the Crimea and reports in the press. When the French experienced difficulties in transporting reinforcements to the Crimea, she offered the use of the royal yacht as a transport for French troops, which could carry 1,000 soldiers. She was concerned for her troops fighting on the battlefields of the Crimea, those that were wounded or killed and for their families at home. In a letter dated 14 November 1854 she wrote:

My whole heart and soul are in the Crimea. The conduct of our dear noble Troops is beyond praise. It is quite heroic, and really, I feel a pride to have such Troops, which is only equalled by my grief for their sufferings. We now know that there has been a pitched battle on the 6th, in which we have been victorious over much greater numbers, but with great loss on both sides – the greatest on the Russian. But we know nothing more, and now we must live in suspense which is indeed dreadful. Then to think of the numbers of families who are living in such anxiety! It is terrible to think of all the wretched wives and mothers who are awaiting the fate of the nearest and dearest to them![68]

Victoria was referring to the Battle of Inkerman on 5 November 1854, when the British Army suffered 2,573 casualties, including 635 killed and several high-ranking officers. The French suffered 1,800 casualties, including 375 killed, while the allies' opponent, Russia, sustained 15,245 casualties, including 3,286 killed. The failure highlighted by the deficiencies in the British Army during the war prompted a complete overall of organisation within the armed service.

---

68. Ibid., p.52.

41

Crimea War Medal

Victoria ordered a campaign medal to be awarded to those who fought in the Crimea.

The Crimean War was fought during October 1853 and February 1856 between the alliance comprising the Ottoman Empire (now known as Turkey), Britain, France and Sardinia against Russia in an effort to stop her expansion along the River Danube through eastern Europe. It was the only European war fought by Britain during Victoria's reign and the first fought on European soil since Napoleon was defeated by the Duke of Wellington at the Battle of Waterloo in 1815.

The war was mainly fought in the Crimea and the Black Sea. The Allied force comprising 27,000 British, 30,000 French and 7,000 Turkish troops landed unopposed at Old Fort near to Eupatoria on 14 September 1854. The primary aim was to then march 30 miles towards Sebastopol, the base of the Russian Navy now called Sevastopol, where it was hoped to destroy the fleet. If this objective was achieved the Russians would be unable to carry out further incursions into the Ottoman Empire and the trade routes between Britain and India would be secured.

The three prime battles during the Crimean War were fought at Alma on 20 September 1854, Balaclava on 24 October 1854 and the Russian offensive at the Inkerman during November 1854.

Victoria read progress reports and listened to generals during the Crimean War. She was concerned for the welfare of her soldiers and appreciated the depravations that they had to endure as they fought for queen and country. She wanted to honour every soldier who fought during the Crimean War with a medal. On 30 November 1854 she wrote of her intentions for Crimea War Medal to the Duke of Newcastle:

> The medal should have the word 'Crimea' on it, with an appropriate device (for which it would be well to lose no time in having a design made) and clasps – like the Peninsular Medal, with the names *Alma* and *Inkerman* inscribed on them, according to who had been in one or both battles. *Sebastopol* should it fall, or any name of battle which Providence may permit our brave troops to gain, can be inscribed on other clasps hereafter to be

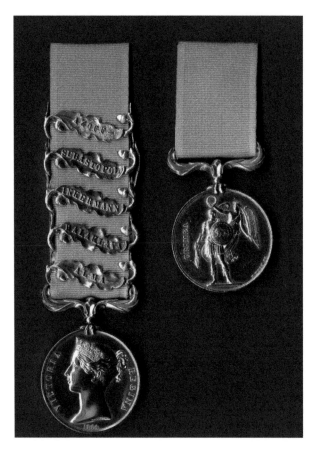

The front and reverse of the specimen sample of the Crimea Medal held by the Medal Office at Innsworth Barracks. It has all the available clasps inscribed with names of the battles; Azoff, Sebastopol, Inkermann, Balaklava and Alma. (Historic Military Press)

added. The names *Alma* and *Inkerman* should likewise be borne on the colours of all the regiments who have been engaged in these bloody and glorious actions. The Queen is sure that nothing will gratify and encourage our noble troops more than the knowledge that this is to be done.[69]

The medal was made of silver, bearing the Queen's head, with the words 'VICTORIA REGINA' and '1854' inscribed on the front, while the reverse depicted a Roman warrior about to receive a laurel from a flying figure representing Victory, alongside the word 'CRIMEA'. The decorative clasps were unusual for they represented an oak leaf with an acorn at each end, a style not used for any other British decoration. The clasps and medal were attached to a ribbon, which was coloured pale blue with yellow edges. Five clasps were authorised: Alma, for the battle of 20 September 1854; Balaklava, 25 October 1854; Inkerman, 5 November 1854; Sebastopol, for the siege that took place from 11 September 1854 to 9 September 1855 (Participants of the actions at Balaklava and Inkerman were eligible to be awarded this clasp); and Azoff, which was awarded to Royal Naval personnel that took part in operations in the Sea of Azoff between 25 May and 22 September 1855.

---

69. Benson, Vol. 3, op. cit., p.56.

42

Brompton Hospital, Chatham

Victoria's first visit to her wounded soldiers.

Distressed by the sufferings of her soldiers fighting the Crimean War, on 3 March 1855, Victoria inspected the military hospitals at Fort Pitt and Brompton Hospital in Chatham to ensure that those who were wounded during that campaign were receiving sufficient medical care when they returned home. The building that was once Brompton Hospital is now the officers' mess at the Royal School of Military Engineering, Chatham.

Among the three hundred patients receiving treatment at the Brompton Hospital, there were sixty-four soldiers who were wounded in the Crimea. Victoria took an interest in each soldier she encountered and inquired about their wounds and their experience in the war. As sovereign, she was unable to visit the battlefield, but visiting military hospitals in Britain was an opportunity for her to assess the quality of the medical treatment of her soldiers. This visit marked a turning point where Victoria rejected protocol and the previous distant relationship between the sovereign and her subjects was abandoned by engaging in conversation to obtain first-hand accounts from those who fought in the war.

Accompanied by Prince Albert and her two eldest sons, Edward, Prince of Wales and Prince Alfred, the royal party was received by Colonel Eden, Commandant of the Chatham Garrison, and Doctor Read, the staff surgeon of the hospital. They visited a ward where twenty-five cavalrymen wounded during the Charge of the Light Brigade at Balaklava were convalescing, including Sergeant Scarff of the 17th Lancers, who had received sabre cuts to his head, hands, back and thigh. In another ward, the Queen met Sergeant John Breese, who lost an arm at the Battle of Inkerman, and after the visit he was appointed to her personal bodyguard. Many of the soldiers found it difficult to stand in respect of the Queen as she entered the wards, but she was mindful of their wounds and advised them to forsake protocol and sit down so they would be more comfortable. Meeting these soldiers deeply affected Victoria, for she wrote that 'the sight of such fine, powerful frames laid low and prostrate with wounds and sickness on beds of sufferings, or maimed in the prime of life, is indescribably touching to us women, who are born to suffer, and can bear pain more easily,

The officers' mess at the Royal School of Military Engineering, Chatham, which was once Brompton Hospital. The latter was visited by Victoria in 1855. (Courtesy of Sergeant Paul Herron)

so different to men, and soldiers, accustomed to activity & hardships, whom it is particularly sad and pitiable to see in such a condition'.[70]

Victoria's visit did raise the morale of the soldiers convalescing in the hospital. Private John King, who served with the 1st Battalion, Rifle Brigade, was among those soldiers. He had been wounded at the Battle of Inkerman. As the Russians temporarily captured the ground on which he lay, he had rubbed blood over his face to feign death. The ruse succeeded and he was evacuated to England. He wrote of the Queen's visit in a letter to his sister:

> All the sick and wounded in the hospitals in Chatham, were delighted a few days after our arrival with a visit from Her Majesty and her Royal Consort. The soldiers were already aware of the deep sympathy which Her Majesty felt for the sick and wounded –

70. Royal Archives: RA VIC/MAIN/QVJ (W), 3 March 1855 (Courtesy HM Queen Elizabeth II).

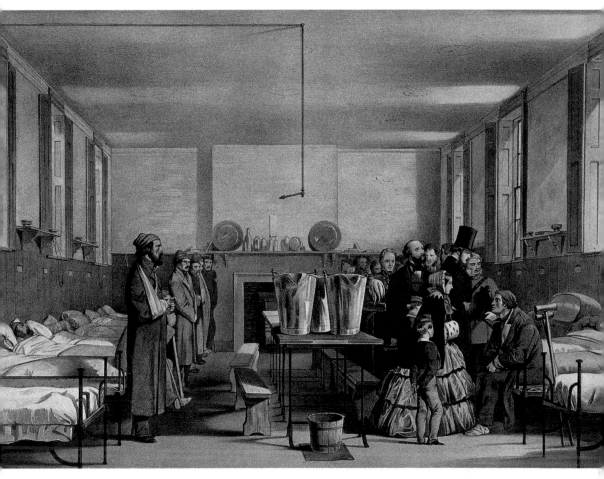

Victoria and Albert visiting soldiers wounded in the Crimean War, at Brompton Hospital, Chatham, on 3 March 1855. (Courtesy of the Wellcome Collection)

her feeling and consolatory letter to Mrs. Herbert, which was read to us in Scutari, almost made us forget all past suffering; and her condescension in personally visiting the hospitals and entering in conversation with us, kindly enquiring into our wants and conditions, has endeared her, if possible, more, than ever in our affections and if we had a thousand lives they would be freely offered in her service.[71]

The royal visit to Brompton Hospital was not just a gesture or a public relations exercise, Victoria was paying attention to the conditions in which her wounded soldiers were being treated. Victoria returned to visit wounded soldiers evacuated from the Crimea at Brompton Hospital on 19 June 1855 and 16 April 1856.

---

71. *Armagh Guardian*, 30 March 1855.

43

Horse Guards Parade

Victoria decorated 768 servicemen from the British Army and Royal Navy with the Crimea War Medal at Horse Guards Parade.

Horse Guards Parade is the ceremonial parade ground in St James's Park and the building known as Horse Guards still remains the official entrance to Buckingham Palace and St James's Park.

It was there on 18 May 1855 that Victoria presented the Crimea War Medal to eligible recipients, establishing a precedent where soldiers of all ranks were decorated with medals acknowledging courage directly from the sovereign, a tradition that has been carried through successive reigns during the past 164 years. The *Morning Chronicle* declared: 'Amongst the many remarkable incidents of her reign, none is more significant than this ceremony … it was still reserved for her to show that if our troops do indeed fight beneath "the cold shadow of the aristocracy", there is no "cold shade" between them and the throne. For the first time in our history the Sovereign has personally distributed to men of every rank the honours that, without distinction of rank, they have won on the same bloody and "well foughten fields".'[72]

Victoria was stirred by her visit to wounded soldiers convalescing at the Chatham Hospitals, to such an extent that it prompted her to take the unprecedented decision to personally present the Crimea War Medal to officers and men who were either wounded or on leave. In a letter to Lord Panmure on 22 March 1855, she wrote that:

the Queen has since thought that the value of the Medal would be greatly enhanced if she were personally to deliver it to the officers and a certain number of men (for that purpose). The valour displayed by our troops, as well as the sufferings they have endured, have never been surpassed – perhaps hardly equalled; and as the Queen has been a witness of what they have gone through, having visited them in their hospitals, she would like to be able personally to give them the reward they have so well, and will value so much.[73]

---

72. *Morning Chronicle*, 19 May 1855.

73. Benson, Vol. 3, op. cit., p.116.

Horse Guards Parade was where Victoria presented the Crimea Medal to recipients on 18 May 1855. The Horse Guards building, with the impressive clock tower built over the archway, was designed by William Kent, chief architect during the reign of King George II in the eighteenth century. (Courtesy of Cristian Bortes)

As well as acknowledging the courage and resilience of her soldiers, Victoria also recognised that such a ceremony would have a positive impact upon recruitment. A platform that protruded from the Horse Guards building was specially built for the royal family and draped with scarlet cloth. Fifty yards from Horse Guards, a dais, adorned with crimson cloth, was specifically positioned on the centre of the parade ground, on which the Queen stood and presented the medals. A gilded chair of state was placed upon this platform for the Queen and a smaller chair for Prince Albert.

The servicemen who were to receive the Crimea War Medal marched through the arch of Horse Guards. Sailors from the Royal Naval Brigade passed through the arch at 9.30 am and received a rousing reception from the spectators as they approached the dais marching behind the Royal Marines Band, which played 'Rule Britannia'.

At 11 am Victoria and her family appeared and stood on the platform, amidst cheers from the spectators as a canon thundered to herald their arrival. *The Times* reported that the Queen 'wore a lilac and white dress, green velvet mantle, and white bonnet, looked extremely well'.[74] Prince Albert wore the uniform of a field marshal. The soldiers who were to be decorated stood before her and comprised detachments from every regiment serving in the Crimea, Cavalry, Guards, Infantry, Artillery and Royal Marines, as well as seamen serving with the Royal Navy.

---

74. *The Times*, 19 May 1855.

Victoria presenting Crimea Medals on Horse Guards Parade, 18 May 1855. (Anne S.K. Brown Military Collection, Brown University Library)

The soldiers then passed along towards the Queen in single file, holding a card bearing their name, rank and if wounded, at what battle, which they handed to Major-General Wetherall. The information was then read out for the Queen's benefit by the Adjutant-General, so that when each soldier stood before her, she knew his name and his deeds, making the experience very personal to that soldier being honoured. Lord Panmure, Secretary for War, passed the medals to the Queen, who in turn presented them to the soldiers. She then kindly spoke to each individual soldier with words of comfort and empathy as she presented the Crimea War Medal.

The ceremony lasted an hour, during which time Victoria decorated 768 officers, soldiers and sailors. A party of 450 of the non-commissioned officers and men from the ranks were marched to the Queen's Riding School, adjacent to Buckingham Palace where they were honoured with dinner, during which Victoria and Albert paid them a visit.

44

Crystal Palace, Sydenham

The exhibition building that had been constructed with glass built to house the Great Exhibition in Hyde Park was dismantled in 1853 and transferred to Sydenham, where it was re-erected and opened by Victoria in a grand ceremony in 1854. It would continue to be known as Crystal Palace. Victoria and her war ally, the French Emperor Napoleon III, visited Crystal Palace on 20 April 1855.

After the closure of the Great Exhibition during October 1851, the fate of the grand Crystal Palace was uncertain. Despite the removal of all the exhibits, the glass building still stood and as Victoria passed it on 22 March 1852, she reflected that 'it brought back so vividly its glories and delights, and the happy, brilliant time of last year, – the excitement concerning its progress and success last year at this time and I felt quite melancholy that it was all past, and this still beautiful and graceful building was to go. I hate the idea of its being taken down, though I realise that it ought to be done.'[75]

It was decided to dismantle Crystal Palace in Hyde Park and relocate and reconstruct it on Sydenham Hill, which was 6 miles away in rural south London. The structure was purchased by Francis Fuller, a member of the Executive Committee of the Great Exhibition, and directors of the Brighton Railway Company for £70,000 (£5.6 million in 2017). The Crystal Palace Company was established in order to preserve the building so it could be enjoyed as a centre of entertainment. A railway line was specifically built to transport visitors from London Bridge Station to the site and a new station named Crystal Palace Station was built. Using the lines that were used to build the railway track in Hyde Park, visitors would arrive at its new location in Sydenham. The crowds would disembark from trains to enter the building through a self-serving turnstile, where they would pay one fee that combined entry to the building and travel from London.

Crystal Palace at Sydenham would become a winter garden, enclosing 18 acres. The central transept was taller than the one built at Hyde Park and two water towers, designed by Isambard Kingdom Brunel, were built either side of the large glasshouse. Ornate fountains were installed in the grounds that could project water 200ft high, which surpassed those at the Palace of Versailles outside Paris. On 10 June 1854, Victoria opened Crystal Palace with pomp and ceremony.

---

75. Royal Archives: RA VIC/MAIN/QVJ (W), 22 March 1852 (Courtesy HM Queen Elizabeth II).

The remains of the terrace at Crystal Palace in Sydenham. (Courtesy of Robert Lamb; www.geograph.org.uk)

During the state visit of Emperor Napoleon III, Victoria took him on 20 April 1855 to Sydenham to view Crystal Palace. The two heads of state were allies and discussed the progress of the Crimean War. Vast crowds of between 30,000 and 40,000 people assembled on the terrace to view the royal party. The public got too close to the party as they walked along the nave of Crystal Palace, to the extent that their space was intruded and they were being touched. The Emperor feared assassination and Victoria, who was anxious, took him by the arm and led him through the crowd.

Crystal Palace was enjoyed by the public throughout Victoria's reign. However, it was destroyed by fire of unknown origin on 1 December 1936. The two towers survived but they were dismantled in 1941 because they were prominent landmarks that could aid German Luftwaffe pilots conducting bombing raids over London during the Second World War. Some of the sculptures, the balconies and a dinosaur park built in 1855 still exist on the site.

45

Order of the Garter

Emperor Napoleon III was installed by Victoria as a Knight of the Order of the Garter in the Throne Room, Windsor Castle, on 18 April 1855 during his state visit to Britain.

The Order of the Garter is an order of chivalry, which was established in 1348 by King Edward III with the aim of creating his own inner circle of knights in the tradition of King Arthur. Edward established St George, a Greek Christian who originated from Cappadocia (now in Turkey), as Patron Saint of England. The Order of the Garter features the Cross of St George enclosed by a garter with the motto 'Honi soit qui mal y pense', which translates as 'Shame on him who thinks of evil of it'. It is regarded as the most senior order of knighthood within the British honours system, except for the Victoria Cross and George Cross, which supersedes it in precedence.

Victoria was responsible for appointing members to the order, which included the Prince of Wales and twenty-four members, or Companions. Prince Albert, French King Louis Phillippe, Victor Emmanuel, King of Sardinia, Franz Joseph, Emperor of Austria and British Prime Ministers Henry John Temple, Third Viscount Palmerston, Arthur Wellesley, the Duke of Wellington, John Russell, First Earl Russell, Benjamin Disraeli, Earl of Beaconsfield and Robert Gascoyne-Cecil, Third Marquess of Salisbury, were all appointed to the Order of the Garter during her reign.

On 18 April 1855, Victoria installed Napoleon III to the order, and the ceremony formed one of the highlights of the French Emperor's state visit to Britain that it was hoped would cement Anglo-French relations. The Crimean War brought Britain and France closer together as they were allied against Russia and Victoria invited the Emperor on a state visit. Victoria invested Emperor Napoleon III as a knight in the Throne Room at Windsor Castle.

The state visit provided an opportunity to discuss the progress of the Crimean War and Napoleon III expressed his concerns at the poor leadership of allied generals. He considered visiting the Crimea personally to prevent a disaster occurring, but Victoria tried to dissuade him. A state ball was held in the Waterloo Gallery at Windsor Castle and, Victoria appreciated the irony and historic significance of dancing with the nephew of George III's enemy Napoleon I:

The emblem of the Most Noble Order of the Garter. (Courtesy of Nicholas Jackson)

How strange to think that I, the grand-daughter of George III, should dance with the Emperor Napoleon, nephew of England's great enemy, now my dearest and most intimate ally, in the Waterloo Room, and this ally only six years ago, living in this country an exile, poor and unthought of! … I am glad to know this extraordinary man, whom it is certainly impossible not to like when you live with him, and not even to a considerable extent to admire. I believe him to be capable of kindness, affection, friendship and gratitude. I feel confidence in him as regards the future.[76]

Victoria entertained Napoleon III at Windsor Castle for three days and on 19 April they all went to Buckingham Palace, when during that evening they went to Her Majesty's Theatre in Haymarket to see *Fidelio*, the opera written by Beethoven. The following day Victoria took Napoleon III to Sydenham to see the Crystal Palace. On 21 April, the Emperor returned to France. The Queen was overwhelmed by the experience and recognised the importance of the state visit and the benefits to Britain.

---

76. Browne, op. cit., p.50.

46

Gold-Enamelled Brooch Presented to Florence Nightingale by Victoria

Sometimes referred to as the 'Nightingale Jewel', this brooch, the design of which was supervised by Prince Albert, was made by R. and S. Garrard & Co. in 1855 and presented to Florence Nightingale by Victoria as a gift to acknowledge her work as a civilian in caring for wounded soldiers during the Crimean War.

The Ottomans provided the British with barracks at Scutari, close to Constantinople, to be used as a base hospital. The hygiene and sanitary conditions of these barracks was extremely poor, making the facility totally unsuitable for use as a medical centre for wounded soldiers. Victoria was concerned about the state of medical care in the British Army. She wrote: 'This is a terrible season of mourning and sorrow, how many mothers, wives, sisters and children are bereaved at this moment. Alas! It is that awful accompaniment of war, disease, which is so much more to be dreaded than the fighting itself.'[77]

Dedicated nurses were required within those military hospitals. Florence Nightingale, a professional nurse with high standards, offered to go the Crimea and co-ordinate the nursing operation.

Despite the poor conditions and being confronted by military bureaucrats, Nightingale succeeded in making adequate changes to improve those conditions. As well as supervising these changes, she regularly carried out rounds through each ward at night, carrying a lamp and giving comforting words to the wounded. She would hence force be affectionately be known as the Lady with the Lamp. One anonymous soldier wrote: 'She would speak to one and another, and nod and smile to many more; but she could not do it all, you know – we lay there in hundreds – but we could kiss her shadow as it fell, and lay our heads on the pillow again, content.'[78]

There was no decoration to award civilians for the work that Nightingale had carried out on behalf of the British Army. Victoria wanted to personally acknowledge her nursing endeavours in the Crimean War, so to show her appreciation, on 20 January 1856, she sent this brooch, which was engraved on the rear with a dedication from Victoria, 'To Miss Florence Nightingale, as a mark of esteem and gratitude for her devotion towards the Queen's brave soldiers, from Victoria R. 1855'. Victoria also wrote the following letter to accompany the brooch:

---

77. Ibid., p.92.

78. Ibid., p.90.

Above left: The gold-enamelled brooch decorated with a red cross and three stars that was presented by Victoria to Florence Nightingale in 1855 for her work in Crimea. (Courtesy of the Wellcome Collection)

Above right: A portrait of Florence Nightingale *c.*1856 that was printed between 1862 and 1877. (Library of Congress)

Dear Miss Nightingale, – You are, I know, well aware of the high sense I entertain of the Christian devotion which you have displayed during this great and bloody war, and I need hardly repeat to you how warm my admiration is for your services, which are fully equal to those of my dear and brave soldiers, whose sufferings you have had the privilege of alleviating in so merciful a manner. I am, however, anxious of marking my feelings in a manner which I trust will be agreeable to you and therefore send you with this letter a brooch, the form and emblems of which commemorate your great and blessed work, and which, I hope, you will wear as a mark of the high approbation of your Sovereign! It will be a very great satisfaction to me, when you return at last to these shores, to make the acquaintance of one who set so bright an example to our sex. And with every prayer for the preservation of your valuable health, believe me, always, yours sincerely, Victoria R.[79]

Victoria invited Nightingale to Balmoral to meet her in person on 21 September 1856. The meeting took place in the drawing room and lasted an hour, during which time the nurse discussed her aspirations to initiate a reform of the military medical services.

---

79. Benson, Vol. 3, op. cit., p.170.

47

Russian Cannon
Captured at Sebastopol

The Crimean War concluded with an armistice during February 1856, followed by the Treaty of Peace signed in Paris during the following month. After the war, many pieces of Russian artillery were brought to Britain as trophies and were presented to various towns across the nation and several cities across the British Empire. A Russian cannon now on display outside Ely Cathedral was presented to the city in 1860 by Victoria as a gift acknowledging the creation of the Ely Rifle Volunteers.

The British Cabinet sanctioned a direct attack upon Sebastopol, home of the Tsar's Black Sea Fleet, on 28 June 1854. The Allied forces landed on the Crimean Peninsula on 14 September 1854 but were unable to capture the port after the initial landing, primarily because of poor leadership and the fact that the Russians had secured the heights that surrounded the base. They had to fight their way across 30 miles of difficult terrain, engaging in three major battles to reach the port. Once the Russians were defeated at the Battle of Inkerman on 5 November 1854, Sebastopol was encircled. The allied nations besieged the port, living in squalid trenches without sufficient supplies and warm clothing. The siege would last for 349 days.

The Russians abandoned Sebastopol on 8 September 1855.

Victoria was pleased to hear the news that Sebastopol had fallen. In a letter dated 11 September 1855, she wrote from Balmoral to Leopold:

Approximately a hundred Russian cannon were captured at Sebastopol, many of which were removed from the ramparts, and there are approximately fifty that were known to have been brought to Britain as trophies. A pair of cannon were sent to several major cities within the British Empire, while others were distributed around the British Isles as a gift from Victoria.

The Russian cannon were not welcomed by some people, including the Kent town of Maidstone. One resident, known as Bread not Bullets, wrote a letter to the editor of the *Maidstone Telegraph* on 30 March 1870. In it he refers to Captain Louis Nolan, who was killed during the Charge of the Light Brigade at Balaklava in 1854, and regarded:

the cannon being rather a disgrace than honour. We were told by one of the contributors that it stood in honour to Nolan. Poor murdered Nolan, the greatest soldier

A Russian cannon that was captured at Sevastopol and which is displayed on Palace Green, close to Ely Cathedral. The cannon was cast during 1802 in the Alexandrovski factory, which was managed by an English director named Charles Gascoigne. (Claudio Divizia/Shutterstock)

in the Crimea. Murdered repeat. Not by the Russians but by the misdirected commands of the British staff. The sooner a veil is cast over the Crimean war the better. Five forces employed to destroy one defence. England, France, Italy, Turkey, and the German Legion, while Odessa was spared – the very place where the Russians obtained their supplies from – because an English Statesman had property there, and directly a British vessel got aground there it was fired upon by the garrison … But, Sir, the time is past for disfiguring our streets with the barbaric trophies of unholy and unchristian war. Do the working classes know that while they are now starving they are compelled to pay 28 million a year for interest alone on our national debt, arising from wars, from which the upper classes alone profit. The world wants peace and plenty, not huge iron cannons to remind them of past follies, which Tories call honour.[80]

80. *Maidstone Telegraph*, 2 April 1870.

48

Victoria Cross Specimen

Victoria was presented with a prototype of the Victoria Cross on 4 February 1856 for her review. The design was die-struck in copper. The design for the suspended 'V', the bar and the reverse of the medal had not been developed.

In early 1856, there were no tangible means of rewarding an individual serviceman, irrespective of them being an officer, or serving in the ranks, or social status, for individual gallantry in the British Army and Royal Navy in any engagement with the enemy. Victoria wanted to establish a medal that recognised individual instances of merit and exceptional valour that would distinguish them from their comrades. Albert suggested that the medal should be named the Victoria Cross. The medal was initially inaugurated for the purpose of recognising individual valour during the Crimean War, for which 111 medals were awarded. However, since it was introduced, the Victoria Cross has been conferred on 1,358 recipients.

Drawings of designs for such a medal were presented to the Queen for her review. She wrote to Lord Panmure on 5 January 1856 to confirm her preferred design and recommended that 'the motto would be better "For Valour" than "For the Brave" as this would lead to the inference that only those are deemed brave who have got the Victoria Cross.'[81]

On 29 January 1856, Victoria instituted by the Royal Warrant the order of the Victoria Cross. A prototype of the medal was presented to Victoria on 4 February 1856 and during the following day this new order of valour was announced in *The London Gazette*. 'The Queen has been pleased, by an instrument under Her Royal Sign Manual, of which the following is a copy, to institute and create a new Naval and Military Decoration, to be styled and designated "The Victoria Cross".'[82] The decoration was intended to be awarded only to those officers or men who, in the presence of the enemy, had performed some single act of valour, or devotion to their country. If it was not performed in the sight of a commanding officer, a junior officer could validate the eligibility. If the recipient performed further acts of valour, a bar could be attached to the ribbon from which the Victoria Cross was suspended. All recipients were entitled to an

---

81. Benson, Vol. 3, op. cit., p.160.

82. London Gazette, 4 February 1856.

Above left and above right: The front and rear of the specimen Victoria Cross that is held for reference by the Medal Office at Innsworth Barracks. (Historic Military Press)

annual pension of £10 per year. Those recipients who received a bar would receive an additional pension of £5 a year.[83]

It has been stated that the bronze material used to produce the Victoria Cross originated from two Russian cannon captured during the siege of Sebastopol, however further research has indicated that the cannon were made in China.

---

83. *The Globe*, 6 February 1856.

49

Balmoral Castle

Balmoral Castle is situated near Crathie in Aberdeenshire. Victoria and Albert completed the purchase of this property in 1852. The old castle was considered too small and on 28 September 1853 Victoria laid a foundation stone for a new castle that was to be built 100yd from the original. After the ceremony the workmen were given dinner, which was followed by dancing and Highland games. The new castle was built using local granite quarried from the estate at Invergelder. Construction of the new castle concluded in 1856. Since it was privately owned by Victoria, Balmoral Castle was not part of the Crown Estate and it has remained a private residence of the royal family since she bought it in 1852.

Victoria first set eyes upon Balmoral Castle on 8 September 1848 when the royal family arrived for a holiday in Scotland. It was during this visit that Lord Aberdeen, the future Prime Minister, who at that time was Secretary of State for Foreign Affairs, offered her the chance to purchase the property, the home of his late brother, the Earl of Fife. Victoria enjoyed the peace, the tranquillity, the beautiful landscape, the solemnity and seclusion from the outside world that Balmoral Castle afforded during her three-week stay. There were no soldiers, and the only guard protecting the royal household at Balmoral was a single policeman.

On 18 September the royal family rode ponies accompanied by estate keeper and gillies, one of which was a youthful John Brown, who would play a prominent role during the Queen's life in the years after Albert died. Although she was on holiday, she was never too far away from matters of state, as she responded to letters and reports relating to international affairs and issues at home. Prime Minister Lord John Russell visited the Queen at Balmoral to discuss political problems in person. She also received Charles Lyell, the geologist, and knighted him at Balmoral. When her holiday came to an end on 20 September, she was saddened to leave.

On 21 November 1848, she decided to purchase the castle. Victoria wrote:

It is a pretty little castle in the old Scottish style. There is a picturesque tower and garden in front with a high wooded hill. There is a nice little hall with a billiard-room; next to it is the dining room. Upstairs, immediately to the right is our sitting-room, a fine large room, and then our bedroom, opening into it a little dressing room which is Alberts. Opposite down a few steps, are the children's and Miss Hildyard's [Governess to the royal children] three rooms. The ladies lived below, and the gentlemen upstairs. After lunch we

The front façade of Balmoral Castle. (Courtesy of Bill Kasman; www.geograph.org.uk)

walked out and went to the top of the wooded hill opposite our windows, where there is a cairn, and up which there is a pretty winding path. The view from here is charming … It was so calm and solitary. It did one good as one gazed around; the pure mountain air was most refreshing. All seems to breathe freedom and peace, and to make one forget the world and its sad turmoils.[84]

Each year, the royal family would return to Balmoral, where they embraced life in the Scottish Highlands. It was here that the Queen felt happy as she was able to spend quality family time isolated from court life in London. There was a small household at Balmoral comprising the Queen's maid of honour, the prince's valet, a cook, a footman and two maids. The Scottish mountains reminded Albert of his homeland. The Queen and her children learnt Scottish dancing. More importantly, the Queen felt comfortable mingling with the local community, including attending dances. There was an essence of freedom that released Victoria from court life. She wrote: 'It is not alone the pure air, the quiet and beautiful scenery, which makes it so delightful, it is the atmosphere of loving affection, and the hearty attachment of the people around Balmoral which warms the heart and does one good.'[85]

It was during annual holidays that Balmoral became a base from where Victoria and Albert would travel around the Highlands incognito, disguised and staying in inns in remote places where they could enjoy privacy. After the death of Albert, Victoria would spend four months each year at Balmoral and it was here that she would establish a close relationship with John Brown. In 1887, Princess Beatrice gave birth to her daughter, Victoria Eugenie, at Balmoral. Victoria received Emperor Nicholas II of Russia and Empress Alexandra there during September 1896. It was during this visit, on 23 September, that Victoria became the sovereign who had reigned longer than any British monarch up to that time.

---

84. Lorne, op. cit., p.208.

85. Browne, op. cit., p.100.

50

The Parade Ground, Hyde Park

The first recipients of the Victoria Cross received the decoration from Victoria on the Parade Ground, Hyde Park.

On 26 June 1857, Victoria decorated sixty-one Victoria Cross recipients at a ceremony at Hyde Park, setting a tradition that would continue throughout successive reigns whereby the monarch would present this prestigious medal in person. Two-thirds of Victoria Cross recipients received theirs directly from the sovereign during the 160 years of its existence.

The day 26 June 1857 was one of firsts, because it was the date of the first ceremony where the first Victoria Crosses were presented and worn, it was the day when Albert was officially recognised as Prince Consort, and this was also his first public appearance after being appointed this title. It was also the first time that Victoria rode horseback during a review of soldiers in London and the first time she sat on her horse, side-saddle, so that she could pin the medals upon the chests of the recipients, who were a lot taller.

The ceremony took place in Hyde Park, close to Grosvenor Gate on the part of the park known as the Parade Ground. It was conducted in the presence of every member of the royal family and 9,000 soldiers. A gallery where 7,000 spectators could watch the presentation ceremony had been built along Park Lane. This faced westwards into Hyde Park and stretched from Hyde Park Corner northwards towards Marble Arch. An article in the *Dublin Times* reported: 'As the troops arrived on the ground about nine o'clock, they were formed in a line about 200 yards in front of this gallery. They stretched across the whole ground, and the variety of the uniforms and the gleam of reflected sunlight that continually danced back and forwards along their helmets, sabres and bayonets, made the whole picture extremely pretty and animated.'[86]

Just before ten o'clock the sixty-one officers and men who were to receive the Victoria Cross marched in single file across the park to where the Queen would present them with the prestigious decoration. They included twelve from the Royal Navy, two Royal Marines, four cavalry, four engineers, five artillery and the remainder from various regiments. There were twenty-five officers, fifteen warrant and non-commissioned officers and twenty-one from the ranks.

---

86. *Dublin Times*, 29 June 1857.

The area of the Parade Ground in Hyde Park, where Victoria presented the first Victoria Crosses.
(Author's Collection)

Victoria and her entourage entered Hyde Park five minutes before her scheduled arrival time at 9.55 am; her entrance signalled by the royal salute from some artillery batteries close by. The Royal Standard was raised at the same time close to the royal pavilion constructed in front of the gallery. The *Dublin Times* described the military jacket that she wore during the ceremony: 'She wore a round hat, with a gold band round it and a red and white feather, at the right of the side. A scarlet body, made nearly like a military tunic, but open some way down from the throat, a gold embroidered sash over the left shoulder, and a dark blue skirt completed the costume of the Queen.'[87]

Victoria entered Hyde Park on horse between her husband, the Prince Consort, wearing the uniform of a field marshal, and Prince Frederick of Prussia, dressed in the uniform of a colonel in the Prussian Army. As the royal party approached the soldiers assembled in Hyde Park, the signal was passed and simultaneously they all presented arms, lowered colours and all the bands played the National Anthem in unison.

Lord Panmure stood at the Queen's side and read the names of each man as they appeared before her to receive their Victoria Cross. Each officer had a loop of cord (red or blue according

87. Ibid.

George Housman Thomas' painting entitled *The Queen distributing the Victoria Cross, Hyde Park*. (Anne S.K. Brown Military Collection, Brown University Library)

to their uniform) attached to the left breast of his tunic, to enable the Queen to fasten the award. Each man stood in line as the Queen stooped from her saddle to present the decoration. The medals were presented in strict order of service precedence and seniority.

Once the twelve recipients from the Royal Navy were decorated, the first soldier serving in the British Army to receive and wear the Victoria Cross was Sergeant Major John Grieve, 2nd Dragoons (Royal Scots Grey).

Victoria wanted recipients of the Victoria Cross to be allowed to bear some distinctive mark after their name denoting that they received the award. She preferred BVC (Bearer of the Victoria Cross), but this would later be shortened to VC.

Victoria conducted the presentation of the Victoria Cross so quietly and expediently that the ceremony was completed within ten minutes.

51

Robe of State

The portrait of Victoria was painted in 1859 by Franz Xaver Winterhalter.

Victoria is depicted wearing the Robe of State and the circlet. The earrings and neckless were produced by Garrard's, the well-known London jewellers, in 1858. The Queen's left hand reposes upon some papers, probably relating to matters of state, adjacent to the Imperial State Crown. The Palace of Westminster, the epicentre of government, can be seen in the background.

The robe of state, also known as the Parliament Robe, consisted of a long mantle worn by the sovereign during the State Opening of Parliament on entering the Palace of Westminster and at the coronation on arrival at Westminster Abbey. The crimson cape, lined with ermine, was 4.5m long and was decorated at the top with two lines of gold lace. It was produced by Ede & Ravenscroft, who has served as royal robe makers since 1689. Such a robe was extremely heavy; the one made for the coronation of Elizabeth II in 1953 weighed 15lb. Concerns about the weight were expressed before the coronation of William IV in 1831, for 'the weight of the King's robes are of such immense weight in gold, that he would infallibly tumble backwards with his gouty legs, if they were ever left for half a minute on his shoulders,' wrote the Honourable George Spencer.[88] When Victoria wore the robe at her coronation and during the state opening of Parliament, it was carried by the eight train bearers. When she opened Parliament in 1866, for the first time since the death of Albert, she refused to wear the robe and it was instead draped over the Sovereign's Throne in the House of Lords. When she sat on the throne, the robe was partially thrown over her left shoulder by Princess Louise. It was reported in *Bell's Weekly Messenger*:

> The only peculiarity in the appearance of the house that excited attention of those familiar with it in former times was the Throne, which was covered, and had all its gilded ornaments concealed, by something that at first glance looked like a white sheet thrown loosely over it. A little enquiry elicited the explanation that the article was no ordinary covering, nothing else in fact than her Majesty's robe of state, which she usually wore on all great occasions

---

88. Wyndham, The Hon. Mrs Hugh, *The Correspondence of Sarah Spencer Lady Lyttleton 1787 - 1870* (John Murray, London, 1912), p.236.

A portrait of Victoria painted in 1859 by Franz Xaver Winterhalter. (Author's Collection)

of ceremonial, but which she could not be persuaded to wear on this, because state and herself were in accord no longer. The robe was there, but the heart to put it on was wanting. There may be some who may feel inclined to criticise the omission, and to judge that if her Majesty consented to sit upon the robe, she might have consented to wear it.[89]

Victoria had reigned Britain for twenty-one years when this portrait was painted in 1859 and it was her fortieth year. Lucknow had been captured by the British in March 1858 and the Indian Mutiny had come to an end. On 1 November 1858, Victoria proclaimed that Britain was an Indian Dominion, which was sanctioned by the Government of India Act in the Houses of Parliament, and for the next eighty years India belonged to the British Empire.

During 1859, Victoria's first grandchild was born to her eldest daughter, Vicky. Frederick William Albert was born in the Kronprinzenpalais (Crown Prince's Palace), Berlin, and Victoria received the joyous news by telegram while she was at Windsor Castle. However, she felt sadness that she could not be in Berlin to be with her daughter and grandson, especially when she learned that the birth was difficult because the baby was in the breech position and nearly died. Wilhelm was affected by the traumatic birth and was born with a paralysed left arm. Victoria's first grandchild would later become Kaiser Wilhelm II. Vicky paid a visit to her mother in Britain in May 1859, but it was not until the following year that she met her grandson in Germany.

---

89. *Bell's Weekly Messenger*, 10 February 1866.

52

Postcard of Victoria and Albert

The royal couple celebrated twenty-one years of marriage during 1861.

Capturing an image became a reality in 1839 when Henry Fox Talbot revealed his experiments in photography. Louis Phillippe I of France was the first sovereign to be photographed, but Victoria also embraced this new technology. The first photograph of a British monarch was taken in 1844 by Henry Collen, who photographed Victoria with the Princess Royal. The Queen commissioned further photographs of her family and household. In 1860, Victoria set a new precedent by allowing photographs taken of her and Prince Albert to be published and made available to the public. She appreciated the new ability for the monarch to connect with her subjects using this medium and is a tradition that is maintained by the current Royal family when official photographs are used to commemorate occasions such as births, engagements, weddings and at Christmas. Images of Victoria and Albert were released during the following year, 1861, the year of their twenty-first wedding anniversary.

Despite being first cousins, the personalities and temperaments of the royal couple were completely different. Victoria was impetuous, sensitive and unpredictable, and capable of becoming tempestuous. Albert was prudent, restrained and rational. Victoria was the dominant one in the relationship, possessing the power and status of queen, while Albert, although intelligent and possessing tremendous administrative and organisational skills, was the junior partner. Despite their differences, they became a successful husband and wife team. Their writing desks were adjacent to each other in their sitting room. Every dispatch that passed through their hands was scrutinised and the prince reviewed and amended documents before them being signed by the Queen.

The marriage of Victoria to Albert lasted for twenty-one years until his untimely death in 1861. The union was filed with love, passion and devotion for each other. Victoria conceived and gave birth to nine children during that time. During the twenty first year of her marriage she wrote to Leopold: 'Very few can say with me that their husband at the end of twenty-one years is not only full of the friendship, kindness, and affection which a truly happy marriage brings with it, but the same tender love of the very first days of our marriage!'[90]

---

90. Browne, op. cit., p.124.

A postcard showing Victoria and the Prince Consort posing together. (Author's Collection)

However, the relationship was placed under enormous stress because they were in the public eye and due to the fact that Victoria was queen and Albert had to be on the sidelines in support. In the eyes of the state and the public in Britain he was not the figurehead of the family or the master of the house. Victoria tried to redress this imbalance during moments when she was photographed by looking up at her husband in adoration and sometimes sitting down below him. However, she was in control.

There were instances when the impulsive Victoria would erupt into a rage, which the passive Albert would have to endure. Victoria acknowledged these tempestuous outbursts in a letter to Leopold. 'Great events make me quiet and calm, and little trifles fidget me and that irritate my nerves.'[91] They made a conscious effort to keep their squabbles and disagreements private and project the image of a happy couple. Despite these outbursts, they would reconcile with each other. The union of Victoria and Albert was regarded as one of the most successful of royal marriages. Prince Albert acknowledged this less than a year before his death:

Tomorrow, our marriage will be twenty-one-years old! How many a storm has swept over it, and still it continues green and fresh, and throws out vigorous roots, from which I can, with gratitude to God, acknowledge that much good will yet be engendered for the world! It is now with these twenty-one years, as with the fourscore years of the Bible, 'if they have been delicious, yet have they been labour and trouble.'[92]

---

91. Benson, Vol. 2, op. cit., p.167.

92. Jago, op. cit., p.358.

53

Queen's Well, Glen Esk

Victoria drank water from this well.

In 1861 Victoria and Albert spent their last holiday together in Scotland, before his premature death at the end of that year. During that holiday they rode 15 miles from Balmoral to Glen Mark, which is above Glen Esk, where they met Lord Dalhousie beside this well and drank spring water from it.

Victoria and Albert, accompanied by their children Alice and Louis and with Jane Churchill and General Grey, passed through the well at Glen Mark. John Brown was among the gillies who escorted them on their journey. They were driven in two carriages to the Bridge of Muick, which spans the River Dee, where six ponies and an additional

The Queen's Well with the Cairngorm Mountains in the background. Representing a stone crown, the monument was erected over a natural spring to commemorate Victoria, who drank from it in 1861. (Courtesy of Trevor Littlewood/www.geograph.org.uk)

pony to carry their lunch awaited them. After riding 15 miles they reached the well, where they were welcomed by Lord Dalhousie. Victoria wrote: 'We remounted our ponies after three and rode down Glen Mark, stopping to drink some water out of a very pure well, called the White Well.'[93]

The royal party continued their journey from this well and travelled a total of 40 miles from Balmoral, arriving at the village of Fettercairn, where Victoria and Albert lodged at the Ramsay Arms inn.

To commemorate Victoria taking refreshment from the well Lord Dalhousie erected a stone monument in the shape of a crown over it. The following words are inscribed on this monument, 'Her Majesty, Queen Victoria, and his Royal Highness the Prince Consort, visited this well and drank of its refreshing waters, on the 20th September, 1861, the year of Her Majesty's great sorrow'.

---

93. Royal Archives: RA VIC/MAIN/QVJ (W), 20 July 1861. (Courtesy HM Queen Elizabeth II).

54

HMS *Warrior*

The first iron-clad warship was commissioned into Victoria's Royal Navy.

By the time shipbuilders introduced armour when constructing ships called ironclads, Britain – which had ruled the waves for centuries – had become worried. In 1859, the first French ironclad, named *La Gloire*, was launched and instilled fear across the Channel because it made wooden vessels obsolete. The Royal Navy's answer to the launch of *La Gloire* was to build its first iron-hulled ironclad, named HMS *Warrior*, which was launched in 1860. When she was commissioned on 1 August 1861, she was 100ft longer than the standard warship of the day and could carry more armament, amounting to sixty guns. At 9,210 tons displacement, *Warrior* superseded *La Gloire*, being 60 per cent larger. She was the largest warship in the world at that time and restored Britain's reputation as a supreme naval power. *Warrior* also represented the transition of naval construction from sail to steam and became one of the fastest ships at that time.

In 1859 Victoria was concerned about the strength of Britain's armed services and despite being allied to France during the Crimean War, she became concerned that it was expanding its army and navy. The French were building the first ironclad warship, *La Gloire*, in Toulon. Prince Albert asked: 'What have we got to meet this new engine of war?'

The First Lord of the Admiralty, Sir John Pakington, was proactive in countering this French threat and had commissioned the construction of a fleet of iron-clad warships in 1859. Isaac Watts, Chief Constructor to the Navy, and the iron shipbuilder John Scott-Russell developed a revolutionary design of iron-hulled warships where the main guns, engine and boilers would be encased in an iron box, protected by 4½in-thick wrought iron plates bolted to 18in of solid teak, which were mounted on the 1in plating of the hull.

The first iron-hulled warship was named HMS *Warrior* and her keel was laid down on 28 May 1859 at Blackwell, London. Construction was scheduled for completion within nine months but delays added a further ten months.

When war erupted in Europe between Austria and an alliance between France and Sardinia in Italy, Victoria wanted an expansion of the Royal Navy greater than intended by her Parliament. On 24 November 1859, the French ironclad *La Gloire* was launched at Toulon. There was now

HMS *Warrior* at Portsmouth Dockyard. (Courtesy of Colin Smith/www.geograph.org.uk)

a race to build *Warrior*. Approximately 2,000 shipbuilders worked through the day and night on shifts to complete the work. The ship was built at a cost of £400,000 (£23.7 million in 2019) which was twice the amount incurred to build a wooden warship.

Warrior was launched on 29 December 1860. At first the hull remained frozen to the slipway after Sir John Pakington had named her and smashed a bottle of wine on her bow. A hundred men ran back and forth across the main deck in an effort bid to dislodge her together with extra tugs and hydraulic rams. After twenty minutes, *Warrior* slid down the slipway into the frozen River Thames. *Warrior* was commissioned on 1 August 1861 and began active service in June 1862.

55

Painting Depicting 'The last moments of HRH the Prince Consort'

The Prince Consort died, aged forty-two.

The year 1861 was the grimmest year of Victoria's life. On 16 March, her mother, the Duchess of Kent, died. As she grieved for her mother, her sadness was further exacerbated by the death of her beloved Albert in the Blue Room at Windsor Castle on 14 December 1861. Victoria would descend into a deep mourning that would last for the remainder of her life.

During November 1861, Prince Albert was feeling fatigued, experiencing stomach problems, suffering from toothache and insomnia, as well as complaining of suffering rheumatic pain in his legs and back. He was also suffering from a cold, when against doctor's advice, he visited the Royal Military College at Sandhurst. This would be Albert's last public engagement and his cold would develop into influenza. He would also have to deal with the scandal that was enfolding around his son, the Prince of Wales. Bertie was sent to Curragh in Ireland to spend time with the British Army as a captain in command of a company belonging to the Grenadier Guards during that summer, to prepare him for his eventual role as sovereign. However, instead of focusing on soldiering, he embarked upon a brief romantic dalliance with an Irish actress named Nellie Clifton. Rumours of the liaison spread across Europe and amongst gentlemen's clubs in St James's in London. When this salacious gossip eventually reached the ears of his parents, they became very concerned and fearful that Bertie was adopting the licentious and debauched behaviour of George IV. Despite his infirmities, Albert visited Bertie at Cambridge, where he was studying at Trinity College, to talk about his conduct and his responsibilities. This conversation took place as they walked in the rain and probably intensified his illness. Bertie was repentant and Albert returned to Windsor Castle on 26 November 1861 feeling confident that his eldest son would behave in the manner befitting a future monarch.

Albert arrived at Windsor Castle extremely ill, and his condition deteriorated. On 1 December, Dr William Jenner, the royal physician, was called to assess Albert's condition and, although he was disappointed to see him feeling uncomfortable, he was confident that he would regain his health. He spent the following night unable to sleep and shivering, which resulted in Jenner

An oil painting depicting the last moments of the Prince Consort. Albert died in the Blue Room at Windsor Castle. Victoria ordered that this room was kept as a shrine to his memory. (Courtesy of the Wellcome Collection)

making a return visit and determining that he might be suffering a temporary fever. Confined to his bed, Albert lost his appetite and continued to suffer from insomnia.

As his condition worsened, he grew weaker but on 14 December 1861 a Doctor Brown called upon him and was optimistic that the fever that he was suffered had receded. He received visits from his children and during the evening he was able to get out of the bed so that the sheets could be changed. However, after needing assistance returning to his bed, he fell asleep and died in the Blue Room at Windsor Castle, the same room where William IV and George IV had died. Typhoid fever and stomach cancer were cited as causes of death.

This was a pivotal moment in the life of Victoria because she then descended into a deep depression that she would endure for the rest of her life. The Blue Room at Windsor Castle was left as a shrine and everything remained in its place as it had been on the day that Albert died until her own death. Her bereavement had a profound effect upon her and she would isolate

The last photograph taken of the Prince Consort. (Author's Collection)

herself from her public duties as sovereign for the next decade. On 20 December 1861, Victoria wrote of her despair and loss to Leopold:

> The poor fatherless baby of eight months is now the utterly broken hearted and crushed widow of forty-two! My life as a happy one has ended! The world is gone for me! If I must live on … it is henceforth for my poor fatherless children – for my unhappy country, which has lost all in losing him – and in only doing what I know and feel he would wish, for he is near me – his spirit will guide and inspire me! But oh! to be cut off in the prime of life – to see our pure, happy, quiet, domestic life, which alone enabled me to bear my much disliked position, CUT OFF, at forty two – when I have hoped with such instinctive certainty that God would never part us and would let us grow old together … is too awful! Too cruel![94]

Victoria kept the royal bereavement private and there was no lying in state nor a state funeral for Prince Albert. The service was a private affair with little pomp or pageantry, after which his body was temporarily interred in the Royal Vault within St George's Chapel, at Windsor Castle on 23 December 1861. During that day, across Britain, flags were flown at half-mast, shops closed and labour was suspended. Money exchanges were closed, leaving their shutters down as a mark of respect.

---

94. Benson, Vol. 3, op. cit., p.474.

56

The Royal Mausoleum, Frogmore

Prince Albert's body was temporarily interred in the Royal Vault at St George's Chapel until a mausoleum was built within Victoria's private estate at Frogmore, half a mile south of Windsor Castle. The mausoleum was built close to the grave of her mother. It was Victoria's wish to be buried within this mausoleum alongside her beloved husband. She laid the foundation stone on 15 March 1862 and the construction was completed towards the end of that year, when Albert's body was transferred there.

The Royal Mausoleum, Frogmore was built to the specific dimensions requested by Victoria to represent the affection and reverence that she and her children felt towards Albert. Robert Wilson provided a detailed description of this sombre edifice:

It is cruciform in plan, the arms of the cross radiating from a central cell, lit by three semi-circular windows in the clerestory, to the cardinal points of the compass. Polished shafts of cold grey granite decorate the outside of the building, and on an octagonal roof of copper a gilded cross gleams on a square-set tower. The transepts are also square, and lit by a clerestory corresponding with that in the central cell. Monoliths of Aberdeen and Guernsey granite flank the steps of the entrance porch, and the whole exterior is faced with polished granites and parti-coloured masonry.[95]

During the morning of 18 December 1862, Albert's body was removed from the Royal Vault at St George's Chapel in a strictly private ceremony in the presence of his sons, Edward, Prince of Wales, Prince Arthur, Prince Leopold (who was nine years old) and his two valets, Löhlein and Maget. Victoria had a restless night at Windsor Castle according to her journal:

Woke very often during the night, thinking of the sacred work to be carried out at 7 o'clock. At that hour the precious earthly Remains were to be carried with all love and peace to their final resting place by our three sons (for little Leopold had earnestly begged to go too).[96]

---

95. Wilson, Vol. 3, op. cit., p.145.

96. Buckle, Vol. 1, op. cit., p.54.

Frogmore Mausoleum, where Albert and, later, Victoria were buried. (Courtesy of Mark Percy/ www.geograph.org.uk)

Victoria's sons carried his coffin to his last place of rest within the Royal Mausoleum, Frogmore, where his body was placed in a sarcophagus. The royal princesses had woven floral wreaths with their own hands and their brothers placed these inside the sarcophagus. Surmounted upon it was a plaster cast of the effigy of Albert, which was at that time being sculptured in marble by Baron Marochetti.

At 1 pm, Victoria and her family, accompanied by members of the royal household, walked from Frogmore House to the mausoleum to pay their respects to Albert in his final resting place. Dr Gerald Wellesley, Dean of Windsor, conducted the service. Victoria wrote:

> dull, raining and mild. Took half an hour's drive with Alice and a quarter to one we all drove down … to Frogmore. Waited a little while in the house, and then walked to the Mausoleum, entering it, preceded only by the Dean. It seemed so like the day at Frogmore, when Albert was so dear and loving. Everyone entered, each carrying a wreath. The Dean with a faltering voice, read some most appropriate Prayers. We were all much overcome when we knelt round the beloved tomb. When everybody had gone out, we returned again and gazed on the great beauty and peace of the beautiful statue. What a comfort it will be to have that near me!.[97]

The Royal Mausoleum became a place of solace and quiet reflection, as she stared at and admired the marble features of Albert's effigy, and Victoria visited it frequently throughout the remainder of her life.

---

97. Ibid., p.54.

57

Victoria's Widow's Cap

After the death of Albert, Victoria mourned his loss for the rest of her life. She would only wear black with the exception of this white cap.

Victoria was aged forty-two when she was widowed and the image of her dressed in black wearing this white widow cap is widely known. Devastated by the death of her beloved husband, she was paralysed with grief and for the following months she sought solitude at Osborne House and Balmoral, refusing to visit Buckingham Palace until a year after his death. Albert died at such a premature age that it was a tremendous shock, for both Victoria and Albert expected to share their lives together into old age. Her world would change forever and she would never recover from that loss. He was her loving, devoted husband, the doting father of their nine children, and he was supportive of her in matters of state and public events. He even remained at her side during her tempestuous moods. He was her rock and Victoria had to adapt to life without him. The happy family life that they both created transformed into sadness. Birthdays and Christmases were no longer joyous events, but moments of painful remembrance that Albert was deceased.

Consumed with feelings of despair and depression, Victoria wore black for the duration of her reign together with this white cap, which she referred to as her 'sad cap', even at the wedding of Princess Alice on 1 April 1862.[98] During the following decade, Victoria was rarely seen in public and this attracted condemnation from politicians, the media and the public, who resented her decision to lead a life in isolation and neglect her duties, which were paid from the public taxes. She led a life of seclusion, however, she still devoted attention to matters of state. Within two weeks of Albert's death, she held a Privy Council meeting on 6 January 1862 at Osborne House.

The Queen was determined to carry out Albert's wishes. Both Victoria and Albert had wanted the wayward Bertie to marry young. Fifteen months after Albert's death, Bertie married Princess Alexandra of Denmark in a lavish ceremony at St George's Chapel, Windsor Castle, on 10 March 1863.

---

98. Royal Archives: RA VIC/MAIN/QVJ (W), 1 July 1862. (Courtesy HM Queen Elizabeth II).

Above left: Victoria's widow's cap. (Author's Collection)

Above right: Victoria photographed while dressed in mourning. (Courtesy of the Wellcome Collection)

The nation was initially sympathetic to the Queen's grief, considering a period of mourning for a year as understandable and respecting her need for privacy during this difficult time. However, towards the end of 1863, Victoria refrained from attending public duties, delegating the Prince and Princess of Wales to attend instead. Newspapers suggested that she should participate in the State Opening of Parliament, but this led her to conceal herself behind the advice given by her physicians, who were under pressure to advise that attending public events would be harmful to the Queen's health. Newspapers were becoming more vociferous, especially *The Times*, which featured an article on 1 April 1864 challenging the Queen for not performing her role as sovereign. She became known as the 'Widow of Windsor' and there were calls for the monarchy to be abolished.

58

Spithead Forts

Four forts built in the Solent are examples of defences constructed during the reign of Victoria.

The unstable political situation in Europe and the development of iron-hulled, armoured French warships prompted the British Government to strengthen the defences around the British coastline and in particular around Portsmouth. It was fearful that while the Royal Navy was defending the British Empire, the coastline could be vulnerable to a French invasion. Also, the modern French warships could bombard Portsmouth with heavy-calibre guns from a distance. Lord Palmerston was a strong advocate for strengthening the defences in the Solent to 'prevent the cradle of our navy from being burnt and destroyed'.[99] In February 1862 a Royal Commission recommended that a ring of steel be built around Portsmouth, which included a series of four forts that would be built in the eastern approaches to the Solent, between Southsea and the Isle of Wight. They were situated on the Horse Sand, the No Man's Land, the Spitbank sandbanks in the Solent and at St Helens. It would take a decade to build them and Victoria would have seen them each time she sailed to the Isle of Wight and when reviewing the Royal Navy at Spithead.

As early as 1846, Lord Palmerston expressed concerns that the English coastline was poorly defended in the event of French aggression, proclaiming that 'our neighbours are kind, civil and hospitable to us individually, but the French nation remembers the Nile, Trafalgar, the Peninsular, Waterloo and St Helena and would gladly find an opportunity of taking revenge'.[100] It was not until 1859 that a scheme was devised to build fortifications in the Solent to protect the eastern approaches and support the land defences around Portsmouth, with estimated costs of £1.5 million (approximately £89 million in 2017). The project was partially approved by Parliament in 1860.

The eastern entrance to the Solent might appear to be wide, but there are sandbanks where at low tide there is only 6ft of water and there were suitable places to construct the four forts, which would eventually be named Horse Sands Fort, No Man's Land Fort, Spitbank Fort and

---

99. *The Times*. 14 August 1877.

100. Ibid.

Spitbank Fort is the closest to Southsea and guards the entrance to Portsmouth Harbour. Together with St Helens Fort, they are smaller than No Man's Land and Horse Sand Fort. (Historic Military Press)

St Helens Fort after the shoals upon which they were built. Work began in 1861 on one of the forts on Horse Sand, north-west of Ryde, but was suspended four months after the Royal Commission made its recommendations because warship design had made hulls impenetrable from cannon shot.

Developments in the construction of heavy guns to target ships were advanced and three years later work began on the Horse and No Man's Land Shoals forts, and on Spitbank in 1867. Concrete blocks were transported from quarries by train and barges and then sunk 17ft beneath the shoals, skilfully guided by divers, to establish foundations. It cost £1 million (approximately £62.6 million in 2017) to build these three forts. They were massive circular structures, chiefly

Horse Sand Fort in the Solent. (Historic Military Press)

built from iron and granite. The granite walls were 15-ft thick and armour plated. The Horse Sand and No Man's Land forts were built to accommodate twenty-four 38-ton guns on the lower tier and twenty-five 18-ton guns on the upper. Spitbank Fort could accommodate nine 38-ton guns and six 7-in guns pointing landwards. The reason why they were pointing in this direction was to counter against a French landing east or west of Portsmouth, then entry to Portsea Island from the north. Spitbank Fort would be able to provide supporting fire to Fort Widley and Fort Nelson, which was built to protect the northern approaches to Portsmouth. St Helens Fort was small and could only hold two 38-ton guns. It took fifteen years to build the forts, but by the time they had been completed the anticipated threat of invasion was non-existent and they would become known as 'Palmerston's follies'. Towards the end of Victoria's reign, the role of these forts was transferred to combatting against light craft and in 1898 searchlights and two 4.7-in guns were positioned on the roof of Spitbank Fort.

The guns were never fired in anger but the forts still stand as a testament to Victorian engineering and as examples of defences constructed to defend Britain during Victoria's reign.

59

Photograph of Victoria and John Brown

Controversy surrounding Victoria's relationship with her servant.

Victoria is photographed with John Brown in the grounds of Balmoral Castle. Brown was born in Crathienard on 8 December 1826 and became a stable boy at Balmoral in 1842 when he was aged sixteen. Victoria first mentioned Brown in her journal on 11 September 1849 and during that year he was promoted to gillie. A gillie was an attendant during a hunting, stalking or fishing trip in the Highlands. In 1851, Brown was appointed the role of leader of Victoria's pony on the recommendation of Prince Albert. Seven years later he became personal gillie to Albert. Brown accompanied the royal family on their great expeditions in the Highlands during the annual holidays at Balmoral in 1860 and 1861.

Victoria's reluctance to appear in public and instead live a life of solitude consumed with grief caused concern amongst her family. In October 1864, Princess Alice, her daughter, discussed with royal physician Dr William Jenner and Sir Charles Phipps, Keeper of the Privy Seal, how they might to extricate the Queen from her depression. It was suggested that John Brown be brought from Balmoral to Osborne House to attend upon the Queen in the hope it would remind her of the happy times that she spent in Scotland.

Brown arrived at Osborne as groom on 20 December 1864 and developed a close relationship with the Queen. By February 1865 Victoria decided to keep him as a permanent member of her immediate staff. She wrote, 'Have decided that Brown should remain permanently and make himself useful in other ways, besides leading my pony, as he is so very dependable.'[101]

After the death of Albert in 1861 and King Leopold of Belgium in December 1865, Victoria had lost the support and love of her husband and her uncle, whom she regarded as a father figure. The strong, assertive male presence of Brown filled the void that had been left by the two men. Brown became the constant personal attendant to Her Majesty on all occasions. He accompanied the Queen on her daily walks and drives, and all her journeys, as well as waiting upon her during banquets. Victoria valued his characteristics of being honest, reliable, trustworthy, discrete and loyal. Their relationship become closer, breaking down the

---

101. Royal Archives: RA VIC/MAIN/QVJ (W), 3 February 1865. (Courtesy HM Queen Elizabeth II).

Victoria, on her horse Fyvie, with John Brown at Balmoral, 1863. (National Galleries of Scotland)

servant–sovereign dynamic, as they became intimate friends. Victoria was a strong advocate of protocol and being reserved, but Brown was the exception, because he took care of her and, more importantly, brought joy into her life. Rumours began to circulate suggesting that they were more than friends and she was referred to by the national press as Mrs Brown. Further supposition was aroused when Sir Edwin Landseer exhibited his painting entitled 'Queen Victoria at Osborne' at the 99th Royal Academy Spring Exhibition, which depicts the Queen mounted upon a pony, with the reigns held by Brown, which is similar to this photograph. Landseer's painting caused the press and public to speculate about her relationship with her servant. The painting attracted large crowds and many were intrigued to see Brown in the painting, which raised his public profile.

Victoria had isolated herself from public life and became dependent upon Brown, who would serve as her personal attendant for nineteen years. She wrote how she valued his service in her book *Leaves from the Journal of Our Life in the Highlands*:

> His attentive care and faithfulness cannot be exceeded, and the state of my health, which of late years has been sorely tried and weakened, renders such qualifications most valuable, and, indeed, most needful upon all occasions … He has all the independence and elevated feelings peculiar to the Highland race, and is singularly straightforward, simple-minded, kind hearted, disinterested, always ready to oblige, and of a discretion rarely to be met with.[102]

Brown saved the Queen when another assassination attempt was made upon her on 29 February 1872. Disregarding his own safety, Brown seized Arthur O'Connor when he pointed a pistol at Victoria as she entered Buckingham Palace, before he could fire it. Brown restrained O'Connor until the police arrived. O'Connor had a paper in his hands, which was a petition for the Fenians, although this was poorly written and had no political significance. After investigation, it was proved that O'Connor acted alone and was insane. Brown was awarded a pension of £25 per annum as acknowledgement for his courage and service.

Brown was known to the royal children as 'the Queen's stallion', but they resented him and felt threatened by the influence that he had within Victoria's court. In May 1901, after Victoria's death, her son Edward VII ordered the removal or destruction of statues, busts and references to Brown. For years he had to tolerate her mother's devotion to her favourite Highland servant, but once she had died, he could now reduce him to the lower status to which he believed he belonged, despite her mother's wish that Brown be treated with respect.

---

102. Buckle, Vol. 3. op. cit., p.664.

60

Photograph Taken of Victoria on 3 April 1866

The Queen is pictured in mourning dress with her dog named Sharp.

Three years after Albert died Victoria continued to live a life of seclusion. Britain had a queen, but she was not carrying out public functions and duties.

By 1866 Government ministers, the national media and the public still appreciated Victoria's suffering, but they wanted their queen to rule the nation and as a response, despite ill health, she began to resume public and ceremonial duties. In February 1866, Victoria was under enormous pressure to open Parliament. In a letter to Prime Minister Lord John Russell she referred to the prospect of attending this event as a 'dreadful ordeal'.[103] She felt coerced by ministers to attend the State Opening Parliament, even though she did not feel ready to appear in public while still grieving for Albert. Although she absolved Russell and his colleagues for requesting her presence, she strongly resented those who were so vociferous in expecting her to carry on and open Parliament. In a letter to Lord Russell on 22 January 1866, Victoria wrote:

> The Queen must say that she does feel very bitterly the want of feeling of those who ask the Queen to go to open Parliament. That the public should wish to see her she fully understands, and has no wish to prevent – quite the contrary; but why this wish should be of so unreasonable and unfeeling a nature, as to long to witness the spectacle of a poor, broken-hearted widow, nervous and shrinking, dragged in deep mourning. ALONE in State as a Show, where she used to go supported by her husband, to be gazed at, without delicacy of feeling, is a thing she cannot understand, and she never could wish her bitterest foe to be exposed to![104]

The letter continued to give comfort to her Prime Minister that she would honour her promise to open Parliament, but she felt aggrieved by the lack of empathy for her situation expressed

---

103. Buckle, Vol. 1. op. cit., p.295.

104. Ibid., p.296.

Victoria and her dog, named Sharp, on 3 April 1866. (Library of Congress)

by the people of Britain and she wrote of her anxieties, her lack of confidence and her state of mind three years after the loss of her husband, as well as dealing with the personal impact of performing this public duty, given that she was grieving:

> She will do it this time – as she promised it, but she owns, she resents the unfeelingness of those who clamoured for it. Of the suffering it will cause her – nervous as she now is – she can give no idea, but she owns she hardly knows how she will go through it. Were the Queen a woman possessed of strong nerves, she would not mind going through this painful exhibition, but her nerves, from the amount of anxiety, and constant and unceasing work, which is quite overwhelming her, as well as from her deep sorrow – are terribly and increasingly shaken, and she will suffer much for some time after, from the shock to her nervous system, which this ordeal shall occasion.[105]

---

105. Ibid., p.296.

61

Statue of Prince Albert, Wolverhampton

Victoria unveiled one of many monuments dedicated to the memory of her husband.

On 30 November 1866, Victoria unveiled a statue dedicated to Albert in Queen's Square, Wolverhampton.

Victoria arrived at Wolverhampton railway station at around ten o'clock during that cold morning. She wrote that 'with a sinking heart and trembling knees got out of the train, amidst great cheering, bands playing, troops presenting arms'.[106] Her entourage entered waiting carriages and they were driven 4 miles into the centre of town, escorted by the 8th Hussars. The streets were decorated with arches, flags, flowers, wreaths and inscriptions. The Queen was overcome by the warm welcome that she received from the people of Wolverhampton, but she was also overwhelmed by being surrounded by so many people while at the same time feeling solitary. She wrote: 'It seemed so strange being amongst so many, yet so alone, without my beloved husband! I felt much moved, and nearly broke down when I saw the dear name and following inscriptions – "Honour to the memory of Albert the good," "the good Prince."'[107]

Anticipating inclement weather, a covered dais had been built especially for the Queen. Before unveiling the statue, Victoria knighted the Mayor of Wolverhampton, which came as a great surprise to him. The covering sheet fell slowly and the crowd cheered as the statue was revealed and the band played the Coburg March. After the ceremony Victoria returned to her carriage for the journey from Queen's Square to Wolverhampton Station. The thirty-minute journey took Victoria through the impoverished districts of the town and she came face to face with those who lived in those areas, who gave her a warm welcome. She wrote.

> We drove back through quite another, and the poorest, part of the town ... There was not a house that had not got his little decoration; and though we passed through some of the

---

106. Buckle, Vol. 1. op. cit., p.879.

107. Ibid., p.879.

A close-up of the statue of Prince Albert that can be seen in Queen Square, Wolverhampton. (Courtesy of Roger Kidd/www.geograph.org.uk)

wretched-looking slums, where the people were in tatters, and many very Irish-looking, they were most loyal and demonstrative. There was not one unkind look or dissatisfied expression; everyone, without exception, being kind and friendly. Great as the enthusiasm used always to be where ever Albert and I appeared, there was something peculiar and touching in the joy and even emotion with which the people greeted their poor widowed Queen![108]

108. Ibid., p.879.

62

Buckingham Palace Garden

Victoria held her first garden party on 22 June 1868.

Victoria set another precedent during her reign by holding the first garden parties in the grounds of Buckingham Palace, a tradition that has continued through to the reign of Elizabeth II. These events give the sovereign the opportunity to meet a diverse range of people from across the nation who have made a positive contribution to their local communities. As she was gaining confidence after seven years of shunning the world as she grieved for Albert, consideration was given to how she was to resume her public duties as sovereign. A ball was deemed inappropriate, but two drawing rooms were held at Buckingham Palace during 1868. A drawing room was a formal court function when ladies were presented at court. These functions were considered too intense and exhausting for Victoria. And instead it was decided to use the garden to host a garden party for invited nobles, officials and fellow royals. The *Dundee Courier* reported on 9 June 1868 that 'two immense tents are being erected in the gardens of Buckingham Palace for the coming garden *fete* or breakfast to be given by the queen. One of the tents will be handsomely fitted up as a drawing room, the other will be appropriated to refreshments.'[109]

Although the event was called 'breakfast', the first garden party in the grounds of Buckingham Palace took place during the afternoon on 22 June 1868 between 4.30 pm and 7.30 pm. Marquees were erected in the grounds where refreshments were served. The band of the 2nd Life Guards and the Grenadier Guards played alternatively during the event. The Queen's private band was also in attendance with Tyrolese singers and these provided entertainment for the six hundred guests. Victoria was accompanied by her children, Bertie, Louise, Arthur and Leopold and Beatrice, and the Duchess of Roxburghe, the Duchess of Wellington, Lady Bradford and Sir John Cowell, Master of the Queen's Household. The Queen entered her garden with some trepidation at 5 pm and began to receive guests in the drawing room tent. After spending the past seven years in seclusion, she found the experience bewildering as she tried to recognise some of the guests. During the event, which lasted for two hours, the Queen talked to some of her guests. It was reported in the *Berkshire Chronicle*:

---

109. *Dundee Courier*, 9 June 1868.

An aerial view of Buckingham Palace showing the gardens at the rear. (Shutterstock)

THE ROYAL 'BREAKFAST' – It is true, as society whispers, that the breakfast given by the Queen in the gardens of Buckingham Palace on Monday week is not to be repeated this year. Rumour had it that there was to be a series of such breakfasts; but there was a misapprehension. It was never intended to give more than one. In addition to the customary state balls and concerts of the season. The entertainment of Monday week certainly gave every encouragement for its repetition on future occasions. Nothing could have been more charming, or more successful everyway. The gardens are remarkably beautiful, and they have in them a little lake, upon which pleasure boats plied, the boatmen being clad in an old-fashioned livery of scarlet. At a distance these boats moving over the water with a freight of bright and various colours, all reflected sharply on the lake, made an exceedingly beautiful scene, surrounded and softened as it was by the tender green of the grass and the trees. The Queen remained for a long time in the garden, looking very well, moving constantly among her guests, and playing the hostess with much animation. It was noticed, too, that there was some little relief on monotony of her mourning dress; she carried a white parasol, for instance. The experiment in short, was gratifying beyond all expectation.[110]

Victoria held a further twenty-five garden parties throughout the remainder of her reign, and the event expanded. Six thousand guests were invited to the party held to celebrate the Diamond Jubilee on 29 June 1887. The last garden party took place on 11 July 1900 and was her last public event.

---

110. *Pall Mall Gazette*, 30 June 1868.

63

Victoria's Saloon Carriage

Example of actual railway carriage used by Victoria during her reign.

Victoria travelled less after the death of her husband, however, her most frequent journeys were made between London and Scotland for private holidays at Balmoral. In 1869 this saloon carriage was built specifically for her at the London & Northwestern Railway (L&NWR) Company Wolverton Works in Buckinghamshire. The carriage is on display at the National Railway Museum, York.

As detailed previously, in 1842, Victoria became the first sovereign to use trains as a means of transport. It was a comfortable, quick and pleasurable experience, which she enjoyed throughout her reign. In 1869, she commissioned two carriages to be built for her personal use at a cost of £1,800 (approximately £113,000 in 2017), and shared the expense, contributing £800 (£50,000 in 2017) to the London and North Western Railway (L&NWR) Company, which was responsible for the construction. The L&NWR was established in 1846 as a result of a merger between the Grand Junction Railway, Manchester & Birmingham and the London and Birmingham Railways. It was regarded as the 'Premier Line' and was a combined stock company.

The carriage was originally built as two vehicles, each with separate six-wheeled vehicles, which were connected by a flexible gangway. This was the first instance of a gangway fitted in Britain, however Victoria felt uncomfortable passing through the two carriages while the train was in motion. Therefore, in 1895 the two carriages were combined into one 60ft-long carriage when they were remounted on a twelve-wheel bogie undercarriage.

This saloon carriage was designed to be luxurious, a home away from home, by Richard Bore using materials chosen by the Queen. It contained her day and night compartments, including a place to sit and enjoy the journey, and sleeping accommodation containing two beds, toilet facilities and accommodation for a servant and her ladies-in-waiting. The sitting compartment had padded walls and ceiling. It was lined with silk.

Victoria's initials 'VR' were embroidered onto the cushions and the carpets. The Queen favoured oil lamps and candle holders in the carriages instead of gas lamps, which were available. The royal arms and the badges of the Orders of the Bath, the Thistle, the Garter

Victoria's saloon carriage on display in the National Railway Museum. (Alamy)

and St Patrick adorned the lower exterior panels of the carriage. The carriage included toilets, however, Victoria preferred to use the conveniences at stations along the route, therefore many stations installed luxurious toilets in case the Queen stopped for a comfort break on her journey.

Victoria used this saloon carriage for the first time on 14 May 1869, during a journey from Windsor to Ballater, which was the closest station to her Balmoral estate. She dictated that her train should travel at 40mph during the day; and then reduced to 30 mph during the night. It is reputed that Victoria had ordered the installation of a special signal on the roof of one of the carriages to instruct the driver to reduce speed if she felt the train was travelling too fast, if she wanted time to view the wonderful scenery of the Highlands or if she wanted to stop the train so that she could eat her meals.

The decorative design of this carriage made it the Queen's favourite and she would use it for thirty-two years until her death, making an estimated 100 journeys during that period. Her last journey in it was on 6 November 1900, from Ballater to Windsor.

64

Blackfriars Bridge

Blackfriars Bridge opened by Victoria.

A statue of Victoria and a plaque commemorates the day when she opened Blackfriars Bridge on 6 November 1869. After spending the entire decade in mourning, her appearance was a rare public occasion.

The bridge opened by Victoria was built on the site of the original, which was opened a hundred years previously in 1769 and named the William Pitt Bridge, after the Prime Minister, William Pitt the Elder. It became the capital's third crossing over the River Thames after London and Westminster Bridges. Repairs were necessary to maintain the bridge; however, after it was planned to renovate the Thames Embankment, it was decided to demolish the William Pitt Bridge in 1860 and build a replacement, which was named Blackfriars Bridge after the Dominican Priory named Blackfriars that stood nearby.

Blackfriars Bridge was completed in 1869 and the Mayor of London invited Victoria to open it, however, she was reluctant to accept. Despite carrying out a small number of public duties during 1868, she was unwilling to carry out a public duty in London of this magnitude. In the view of her private secretary, General Grey, the Queen had been childish and selfish, lacking motivation to conduct royal duties in public. Grey, her children and Prime Minister William Gladstone attempted to persuade her to open Blackfriars Bridge, but she refused to do it in the summer heat. She would also use the excuse that it was too cold in the winter to attend the state opening of Parliament in ceremonial robes as a reason not to attend that event. Gladstone persevered and she eventually agreed to attend the ceremony to open the bridge and the Holborn Viaduct. News that Victoria would visit the City of London to attend these ceremonies was announced in October 1869 and it was rumoured that political agitators were plotting to line the procession route alongside the unemployed as a protest. The Fenians, a republican organisation attempting to establish an independent Ireland, made an unsuccessful attempt to revolt against the British in 1867 and there were rumours circulating that they would attempt to disrupt the events, which would cause Victoria further anxiety. Despite these threats, the Queen opened Blackfriars Bridge on 6 November 1869 without incident:

Blackfriars Bridge today. (Author's Collection)

At 12 o'clock we reached Blackfriars Bridge, the first portion of which was entirely covered in; here, on a platform, with raised seats and many people, stood the Lord Mayor, who presented the sword, which I merely touched, and he introduced the engineer Mr Cubitt (son of the eminent Sir William Cubitt, well-known to my dearest Albert) and another gentleman. I was presented with an address and a fine illuminated book, describing the whole. The bridge was then considered open, but neither I, nor the Lord Mayor, said so. This however has not been found out. The Lord Mayor, Mr Bruce [the Home Secretary], etc. hurried off to their carriages, during which time there was rather an awkward pause and we were well, but very kindly stared at, and continually cheered. I was able to say a few words to Mr Cubitt. At length we moved on, preceded by the Lord Mayor and Sheriffs and some of the Aldermen which led to very frequent complete stoppages.[111]

Although the opening of Blackfriars Bridge was a traumatic experience for the reclusive queen, the event would help increase her popularity among her people and it raised her spirits. Victoria recorded the warm reception that she received from all Londoners, including the affluent and the poor, as she concluded her journal entry by writing:

I never saw more enthusiastic, loyal, or friendly ones and there were numbers of the very lowest. This, in the very heart of London, at a time when people were said to be intending to do something and were full of all sorts of ideas, is really very remarkable. Felt so pleased and relieved that all had gone off so well. Nothing could have been more gratifying. But it is a hard trial for me all alone, with my children, in an open carriage, amongst such thousands.[112]

111. Buckle, Vol. 1. op. cit., pp.630–1.

112. Ibid., pp.630–1.

Above: The plaque commemorating the opening of Blackfriars Bridge, which is located on the north-eastern side. (Author's Collection)

Right: The statue of Victoria that stands on the northern side of Blackfriars Bridge. (Author's Collection)

A statue of Victoria was erected at the north end of Blackfriars Bridge in 1896, twenty-six years after she opened it. Gilded lettering is inscribed upon the front of the plinth with the words 'Victoria R.I. 1896', which an abbreviated for the Latin 'Victoria Regina Imperatrix', meaning, Victoria, Queen Empress. On the rear of the plinth, the following words are written: 'Presented to the citizens of London by Sir Alfred Seale Haslem in token friendship to themselves and loyalty to Her Majesty Queen Victoria.' Victoria visited the City of London on 8 March 1900 and paused at Blackfriars Bridge to gaze at her statue.

65

Charles Dickens Statue, Portsmouth

Victoria received the eminent author for a private audience at Buckingham Palace on 9 March 1870.

The novels of Charles Dickens were read by Victoria, who admired his work and regarded him as one of her favourite novelists alongside Sir Walter Scott and George Eliot.

The first instalments of Dickens' *Oliver Twist* were published in 1837, during the year Victoria ascended the throne, and it was through reading this serial that she became more aware of the deprivations of the poor in the realm that she reigned. Dickens' detailed descriptions of the squalid and impoverished existence of the less affluent in Victorian society acted as a prism to polarise their plight and raise awareness among the ruling classes. Socially conscious of the injustices in Victoria's Britain, Dickens' empathy radiated throughout his novels and would help bring about reforms.

Victoria was an avid reader of Dickens' work and she mentioned his novels several times in her journal. Ever since those early days of her reign she had expressed a desire to make the acquaintance of the renowned novelist, but Dickens was wary of patronage and was reluctant to meet his sovereign.

Victoria made another attempt the following year, when she requested to hear Dickens read *A Christmas Carol.* Dickens wrote: 'I was put into a state of perplexity.' [113] Dickens responded to Colonel Phipps at Buckingham Palace with the words: 'I should assure him of my desire to meet any wish of her Majesty, and should express my hope that she would indulge me by making one of some audience or other, for I thought an audience necessary to the effect. Thus it stands, but it bothers me.'[114] Victoria did not get the opportunity to hear Dickens read *A Christmas Carol.*

The author eventually met Victoria in 1870 at Buckingham Palace. On his last American tour, he had acquired some photographs of American Civil War battlefields. Victoria had a strong interest in this subject and was keen to see the images. On hearing of this from Arthur

---

113. Ibid., p.382.

114. Ibid., p.382.

By Martin Jennings, this statue of Dickens was unveiled in the presence of forty of his descendants in Guildhall Square, Portsmouth, on 7 February 2014. (Courtesy of Tim Spriddell)

Helps, Clerk of the Privy Council, Dickens immediately sent the photographs to the palace. Victoria then invited Dickens to attend so that she could thank him in person.

The meeting took place on 9 March 1870. Victoria wrote: 'I saw Mr Helps this evening at half past six, who brought and introduced Mr Dickens, the celebrated author. He is very agreeable, with a pleasant voice and manner. He talked of his latest works, of America, – the strangeness of the people there, – of the division of classes in England, which he hoped would get better in time. He felt sure that it would come gradually.'

The audience ended when Victoria presented Dickens with a copy of book *Highland Journals* that included the autographed dedication 'To Charles Dickens, the humblest of writers would be ashamed it to one of the greatest'.[115]

The Queen offered Dickens a baronetcy in recognition for his literary achievements, but he declined the honour. When he died three months later on 9 June 1870, Victoria wrote that 'he is a very great loss. He had a large, loving mind and the strongest sympathy with the poorer classes. He felt sure that a better feeling, and much greater union would take place in time. And I pray earnestly it may!'[116]

115. Ibid., p.383.

116. Buckle, Vol. 2. op. cit., p.21.

66

Royal Albert Hall

Iconic entertainment venue opened in honour of Prince Albert.

Victoria was determined that her husband would never be forgotten. The Royal Albert Hall was built to honour him close to the site where his greatest achievement, the Great Exhibition, was held and near to the museums at South Kensington that were funded by profits from the event. It would become an iconic building in London, being used as a concert hall. On 29 March 1871, the Prince of Wales opened the Royal Albert Hall in the presence of the Queen.

Albert had aspirations of establishing a series of buildings at Kensington Gore, south of Hyde Park, as a centre promoting art and science. This area would be known as Albertopolis and, using profits earned by the successful Great Exhibition held in 1851, the Exhibition's Royal Commission purchased Gore House (which once stood where the Royal Albert Hall now stands). Albert did not live to see his plan come to fruition, but after his death it was planned to continue with his ambition. The Royal Albert Hall was originally going to be called the Central Hall of Arts and Sciences and be used as a venue for scientific and artistic conferences, music concerts, art exhibitions and functions promoting agriculture, horticulture and industry; all causes that interested the late Prince Consort. On 29 May 1867, Victoria laid the foundation stone in the presence of her family, Lord Derby, Prime Minister, and Benjamin Disraeli, Chancellor of the Exchequer. It was a rare public outing for the Queen and it was during this ceremony that she announced that the name of the building would be changed, dedicated to the memory of her husband. In front of 7,000 spectators she said:

> It has been with a struggle that I have nerved myself to a compliance with the wish that I should take part in this days ceremony; but I have been sustained by the thought that I should assist by my presence in promoting the accomplishments of his great designs, to whose memory the gratitude and affection of the country are now rearing a noble monument, which I trust may yet look down on such a centre of institutions for the promotion of Art and Science as it was his fond hope to establish here. It is my wish that

Right: An aerial view of the Royal Albert Hall and Hyde Park, where the Great Exhibition was held. (Karen McGaul/Shutterstock)

Below: The main auditorium of the Royal Albert Hall. (Willy Barton/Shutterstock)

this hall should bear his name, to whom it will have owed its existence, and be called 'The Royal Albert Hall of Arts and Sciences'.[117]

A flourish of trumpets and the booming sound of twenty-one guns in Hyde Park signalled the moment when a polished block of granite was lowered into place. Victoria struck it with an ivory hammer and declared the foundation stone firmly fixed.

The Government funded the building of the Royal Albert Hall at a cost of £200,000 (approximately £12.5 million in 2017). It was built in the shape of an ellipse using Farnham bricks and buff-coloured terracotta. A frieze 6ft 6in wide and 800ft long is displayed around the entire circumference of the exterior, which features emblematic groups representing the different branches of art, mechanics and science. These were created by female students at South Kensington schools using buff mosaic on a chocolate background. This massive amphitheatre was modelled on the Coliseum in Rome and was covered by a dome. Victoria detailed the opening of the Royal Albert Hall in her journal:

A little after twelve, started in nine dress closed carriages … for the Albert Hall, for its opening. I drove with dear Alix and Ernest Coburg [Prince Albert's brother]. Immense and very loyal crowds out. Bertie received us at the door and then we walked up the centre of the immensely crowded Hall (8,000 people were there), which made me feel quite giddy. Bertie read the address from the dais, to which we had been conducted, very well, and I handed to him the answer, saying 'In handing you this answer I wish to express my great admiration of this beautiful Hall, and my earnest wishes for its complete success.' This was greatly applauded. The National Anthem was sung, after which Bertie declared the Hall open.[118]

The Royal Albert Hall would transform South Kensington into the great arts centre of the nation. Together with the surrounding museums and colleges, it continues to be an epicentre of art and culture a hundred and fifty years after its completion.

---

117. Wilson, Vol. 3, op. cit., p.292.

118. Buckle, Vol. 2. op. cit., p.126.

67

Deckhouse from the Royal Steam Yacht *Alberta*

The *Alberta* collided with the schooner *Mistletoe* in the Solent while Victoria was aboard on 18 August 1875.

The deckhouse from the Royal Steam Yacht *Alberta* is displayed at Osborne Beach. The *Alberta* was built by the Admiralty at Pembroke Dock in 1863 and launched during the following year. It was a replacement for the *Fairy*, which was a tender to the Royal Yacht *Victoria and Albert*. The *Alberta* was frequently used to transport Victoria from the mainland across the Solent to the Isle of Wight when she stayed at Osborne House. After her first passage on the *Alberta*, she described the vessel as being 'very comfortable, steady and fast quite like a small *Victoria and Albert*'.[119] The *Alberta* had two deckhouses. The one displayed at Osborne Beach was the foreword deckhouse.

On 18 August 1875, Victoria, accompanied by Princess Beatrice and Prince Leopold, began their journey to Balmoral when they boarded the *Alberta* at Osborne around 6 pm and steamed towards Clarence Victualling Yard at Gosport, escorted by the Royal Yacht *Victoria and Albert*. The Queen's nephew, Ernst Leopold, Prince of Leiningen, commanded the *Alberta*. The routine forty-minute crossing was interrupted when the *Alberta* collided with the *Mistletoe* owned by Manchester banker Edward Heywood. Some of the yachts in the Solent sailed close to the *Alberta* in the hope that those on board could get a glimpse of the Queen. A seaman named Brown was just about to dip the ensign on the *Mistletoe* to salute the Queen when the *Alberta*, steaming at 14 knots, struck the *Mistletoe* along the starboard side abreast the mainmast, close to Stokes Bay. A number of the crew from the *Alberta* and *Victoria and Albert* leapt into the Solent to rescue the occupants of the *Mistletoe* that were thrown overboard by the collision. Victoria wrote:

> The evening was very fine, so bright and no wind … When we reared Stokes Bay, Beatrice said, very calmly 'Mama, there is a yacht coming against us,' and I saw the

---

119. Royal Archives: RA VIC/MAIN/QVJ (W), 25 August 1864. (Courtesy HM Queen Elizabeth II).

The deckhouse of HMY *Alberta*. (Author's Collection)

tall masts & large sails of a schooner looming over us. In an instant came an awful, most terrifying crash, accompanied by a very severe shake and reel …[120]

The *Alberta* had cut the *Mistletoe* in two and she sank within three minutes. Victoria recalled:

It all only took only a few seconds, and when I enquired to whom the yacht belonged, was told she had gone down! In great distress I said, 'take everyone on board', repeating this several times. I then went forward, to where all the excitement had been going on and was horrified to find not a single vestige of the yacht, merely a few spars & deck chairs floating about. Two boats were moving round, & we saw one of our men swimming about with a life belt & one poor man in the water, who was pulled into the barge, nearly drowned, with his face quite black. I saw no others in the water, but on deck three or four yachtsmen, also a lady, looking anxiously from one side to the other. These had jumped across from the sinking yacht on to the '*Alberta*'. At first it was hoped that everyone had been saved, and General Ponsonby said the numbers were being counted. Alas! then it

---

120. Buckle, Vol. 2. op. cit., pp.417–20.

became clear that one lady, whom Leopold had distinctly seen on the deck with the other, was missing, also one man, a dreadful moment. I was asked to leave the forepart of the ship, as two poor men were being brought up and the sight was very distressing. However, from near the paddle wheel I could see the poor man being lifted out of the water and lying on the deck, with his coat off and his face perfectly black, Dr McEwan and 2 sailors bending over him & moving his arms backwards & forwards. But he gave no sign of life. He was the Captain or Master of the 'Mistletoe', as the yacht was called, a big man of at least seventy.[121]

In total, three lives were lost, including the master, Thomas Stokes, and Annie Peel (Heywood's sister-in-law), as a result of the collision. The owner of the *Mistletoe*, Mr Heywood, was recovered from the sea. Despite being shaken and traumatised by the experience, Victoria and her entourage continued their journey to Balmoral.

The incident caused consternation amongst the yachting community in the Solent, who believed that the Prince of Leiningen had been responsible for this catastrophic accident, however, the Admiralty refused to try the prince by court martial. Instead, his navigating officer was found to be responsible, which caused a public outcry. It was further inflamed when General Sir Henry Ponsonby, the Queen's Private Secretary, on behalf of the Queen, sent a letter to the Marquis of Exeter, president of the Cowes Yacht Club, instructing all its members not to approach the royal yacht too closely when the sovereign was aboard. The yachtsmen interpreted this letter as the Queen trying to exonerate her officers and demonstrating that the officers commanding the royal yachts disregarded the navigational rules of the road. Two coroners' inquests were held regarding the collision. The first jury could not reach a conclusion, while the second jury brought a verdict of accidental death, condemning the officers aboard *Alberta* for steaming too fast and for not maintaining a proper lookout. However, the officers aboard *Alberta* received no punishment.

The *Alberta* played a prominent role in the funeral of Victoria when her body was transferred from Osborne House to the mainland. Her coffin was placed aboard the yacht on 1 February 1901, beneath a canopy upon the aft deck. The *Alberta* led a procession through the Solent where the Royal Naval Fleet lay anchored and she received a gun salute as she passed each ship. The coffin remained aboard *Alberta* at Gosport overnight before it was conveyed to London for the funeral service the following day. Edward VII continued to use the *Alberta* until she was broken up in 1913. The deckhouse was retained and brought to Osborne House for display in the 1970s.

---

121. Ibid., pp.417–20.

68

Travancore Ivory Throne

Victoria is proclaimed Empress of India.

Victoria had expressed a desire to be known as Empress of India, and there were personal reasons why she wanted an imperial title. There were three emperors in Europe: the Russian Tsar, Alexander II, Emperor Franz Joseph of Austria and Emperor Wilhelm I of Germany, who was the father-in-law of her eldest daughter, Vicky. One day Vicky would become empress, therefore Victoria sought the same title. Potential Russian expansion towards India was a major political reason to elevate Victoria to the status of empress. Despite difficulties in passing the Royal Titles Bill through Parliament, it was passed after a second reading in the House of Commons on the condition that the Queen's title of 'empress' would only refer to India. On 1 May 1876, Prime Minister Benjamin Disraeli proclaimed Victoria as Empress of India, which would reinforce Britain's position as an imperial power on the international stage. For the first official photograph, Victoria insisted on sitting on the Travancore ivory throne.

The Travancore ivory throne in Windsor Castle. (J. Helgason/Shutterstock)

The Travancore ivory throne was presented to Victoria by the Martanda Varma, Maharajah of Travancore, in southern India, in 1851. The throne and footstool is upholstered in green velvet, decorated with Indian and European emblems and adorned with rich gemstones. Two elephants are elaborately carved at the end of both arm rests. This magnificent throne formed the centrepiece of the Indian sector in the Great Exhibition in 1851 and was noticed and admired by Victoria when she visited. The Maharajah's gift would help promote the ivory carving skills of Travancore. Prince Albert sat on this chair during the closing ceremony of the Great Exhibition on 15 October 1851.

When Victoria became Empress of India in 1876, she wanted to be pictured seated in this chair for her official photograph at Windsor.

The official proclamation of Victoria took place in Delhi on 1 January 1877. Victoria could now be called empress and going forwards signed documents as 'V.R. & I', *Victoria Regina et Imperatrix.*

Travancore ivory throne exhibited at the Great Exhibition. (Courtesy of the British Library)

69

Hughenden Manor

Victoria visited Prime Minister Benjamin Disraeli, Lord Beaconsfield, at his country home in 1877.

Benjamin Disraeli was a successful novelist and a prominent and influential politician during the nineteenth century. He had written, *Coningsby*, which focused upon political parties of the time, containing characters bearing similar resemblance to politicians of that day; *Sybil* was a book about life among the working classes and *Tancred* addressed the role of the Church of England in the government of the people. These three books provided a picture of life in Britain and the character of its people during the early years of Victoria's reign. Disraeli served as Prime Minister for two terms and was favoured by Victoria.

Disraeli became a Conservative Member of Parliament for Maidstone during the first Parliament of Victoria's reign in 1837. Victoria had referred to him as 'that dreadful Disraeli'[122] in 1846 and she was not initially enamoured by him when he was appointed Chancellor of the Exchequer in Lord Derby's administration in 1852, writing that 'the country can have no confidence in men like Disraeli'[123]. However, when he served as Prime Minster, during two terms, from February to December 1868 and in 1874–80, her attitude towards him changed and their relationship grew closer; she would later refer to him as 'Dizzy'. They both came from different backgrounds; Victoria being born into a life of royalty and privilege, while Disraeli did not belong to the aristocracy, was not educated at public school and did not serve in the military. In Victoria's words, he had 'risen from the people'.[124]

Victoria had only bestowed the privilege of visiting three of her previous Prime Ministers at their homes: Lord Melbourne, Sir Robert Peel and the Earl of Aberdeen. In 15 December 1877, Victoria paid a visit to Disraeli at his home in Hughenden. The journey from Windsor to High Wycombe took forty-five minutes by train. On arrival at High Wycombe Station she was

122. Royal Archives: RA VIC/MAIN/QVJ (W): 26 June 1846. (Courtesy HM Queen Elizabeth II).

123. Royal Archives: RA VIC/MAIN/QVJ (W): 17 December 1852. (Courtesy HM Queen Elizabeth II).

124. Royal Archives: RA VIC/MAIN/QVJ (W): 27 February 1868. (Courtesy HM Queen Elizabeth II).

Above left: The entrance to Hughenden Manor, country home of Benjamin Disraeli, Earl of Beaconsfield. (Author's Collection)

Above right: The library at Hughenden, in which Disraeli hosted Victoria when she visited him on 15 December 1877. (Author's Collection)

welcomed by Disraeli and the local mayor, from where they were transferred to Hughenden. After welcoming the Queen at the station, Disraeli sped ahead of her so he could welcome her once again, but at the entrance to his home. She recalled:

> Hughenden, which stands in a Park, rather high, and has a fine view. Lord Beaconsfield met me at the door, and led me unto the Library, which opens on to the terrace & a pretty Italian garden, laid out by himself. We went out at once, and Beatrice and I planted each a tree, then I went back into the Library and he gave me an account of yesterday's Cabinet, which had been very stormy.[125]

Victoria spent two hours with Disraeli before departing for Windsor Castle. Despite losing the general election in March 1880, Disraeli returned to Hughenden, where he resumed writing his novel *Endymion*, which he had stopped working on in 1872. He completed this final novel in November 1880, but his health had been failing for a number of years as he suffered from asthma and gout.

---

125. Buckle, Vol. 2. op. cit., p.577.

70

Engraving of Victoria and Members of the Royal Family

During their marriage, Victoria produced and raised nine children, many of whom would marry into the royal families of other European nations. These marriages produced thirty-nine grandchildren, including seven heads of state, establishing Victoria as the 'matriarch of Europe'. This engraving published in 1877 shows Victoria and her extensive family.

Victoria always took an interest in foreign affairs, but as her family increased, her family connections personally interlinked her with most of the royal houses in Europe. Analysing some of the European nations and how Victoria was linked shows the considerable influence that she had. Disraeli proclaimed his sovereign as the 'mother of many nations'.[126]

In Germany, Victoria was strongly connected with the German royal household. Her mother was a Princess of Saxe-Coburg before she married her father and became the Duchess of Kent. Her husband was Prince Albert of Saxe-Coburg. Her sons-in-law were Emperor Frederick III of Germany, who married the Princess Royal in 1858, Prince Henry of Battenberg, who married Princess Beatrice in 1885; Prince Louis, the Grand Duke of Hesse, who married Princess Alice in 1862, and Prince Christian of Schleswig-Holstein, who married Princess Helena in 1866.

As mentioned previously, King Leopold I of Belgium was Victoria's uncle and was an influential figure during Victoria's life. His wife was the daughter of French King Louis Phillippe; her cousin, Princess Victoria of Saxe-Coburg, married the Duc de Nemours, son of Louis Phillippe.

Victoria was connected with the Russian royal family when during 1874, her son, Alfred, Duke of Edinburgh, married Grand Duchess Maria Alexandrovna of Russia, a daughter of Czar Alexander. Princess Alice's daughter Alexandra (Victoria's granddaughter) married Czar Nicholas II in 1894. She was executed with her husband and family in 1918 after being usurped during the Russian Revolution the previous year.

In Holland, Victoria's daughter-in-law, the Duchess of Albany, who married her son Leopold in 1882, was the sister of the Queen of Holland. Her daughter-in-law, the Princess of Wales, who married Bertie in 1866, was the daughter of the King of Denmark. Her cousin Ferdinand

---

126. Ponsonby, op. cit., p.63.

A contemporary print of Victoria with other members of the Royal family. It was published on 14 July 1877. (Library of Congress)

of Saxe-Coburg married the Queen of Portugal and fathered two successive kings. Victoria's cousin, Augustus of Saxe-Coburg, was father of Prince, later King, Ferdinand of Bulgaria. Three of Victoria's granddaughters would become the queens of Greece, Romania and Spain.

Towards the end of Victoria's reign, her family had expanded significantly. At the time of her death in 1901, she was the grandmother to thirty-one grandchildren and she was the great-grandmother to thirty-seven great grandchildren. Emperor Wilhelm II of Germany, Emperor Nicholas II of Russian and the future King George V were among her grandchildren. Victoria would embrace the role of grandmother and great-grandmother, becoming one of the most formidable matriarchs in royal history. Wilhelm respected and feared his grandmother and it is believed that if Victoria had lived into her nineties, she would have had the gravitas, strength and influence to instruct her grandson to keep the German Army out of Belgium in 1914 and the First World War may not have happened during that year.

71

Royal Victoria Hospital, Netley

The Royal Victoria Country Park near Southampton stands on the site of the Royal Victoria Netley Hospital. Victoria visited soldiers wounded at Rorke's Drift during the Anglo-Zulu War at the hospital on 11 August 1879 and decorated Private Hitch with the Victoria Cross.

The Royal Victoria Hospital was built after the Crimean War specifically for tending to wounded soldiers and to train doctors and nurses. It was regarded as the largest military hospital in the world. Built alongside the eastern bank of Southampton Water, it was close to Southampton where ships from across the British Empire could disembark wounded service personnel. It also enabled Victoria to make regular visits to the hospital, which was named after her, when she was residing at Osborne House.

Victoria laid the first foundation stone of Netley Military Hospital on 19 May 1856. She wrote: 'Loving, my dear, brave army as I do and having seen so many of my poor sick and wounded soldiers, I shall watch over this work with maternal anxiety.'[127] Netley Hospital was built on a 100-acre site and could accommodate 1,000 patients in wards of varying sizes. Additional barracks were also built to accommodate 1,000 soldiers who were convalescing. A jetty was built on Southampton Water to enable military vessels to disembark the wounded. The hospital received its first patients on 19 May 1863.

Once the military hospital was constructed, Victoria would make eleven trips to visit soldiers recovering from wounds sustained during the wars that were fought during the latter part of her reign. One of those visits took place at 5.15 pm on 11 August 1879, when Victoria and Princess Beatrice disembarked from the *Royal Yacht Alberta* into a rowing boat that took her to Netley Pier. The entire 570ft length of Netley Pier was carpeted in preparation for the royal visit. The Queen was escorted through the wards by Surgeon Generals Massey C.B, and Longmore C.B. and she was initially introduced to soldiers that were suffering from fever and dysentery who had been returned from the Anglo-Zulu War in Natal and a small number from India. She gave some quiet words of comfort.

However, there was a special purpose for Victoria's visit on that day. Just before she left the hospital, hundreds of patients and soldiers from the Army Service Corps and Army Hospital Corps were assembled in a square in front of the steps of the grand entrance. The name of

127. Wilson, Vol. 2, op. cit., p.694.

The chapel in the former grounds of the Royal Victoria Hospital at Netley. This building is all that remains of the site, much of which is today a park. (Courtesy of Tim Firkins)

'Private Hitch' was called out by the Commandant in a firm voice. The unsuspecting Private Frederick Hitch was unaware that he would be receiving the decoration of the Victoria Cross personally from the Queen. He had been wounded during the action at Rorke's Drift on 22 and 23 January 1879 while defending the burning hospital while the patients were evacuated to the safety of the fort. He sustained a serious wound to his shoulder that impeded the use of his right arm. Hitch was one of eleven Victoria Crosses awarded for this action. Hitch was dressed in blue serge coat, the uniform of a patient, with his arm in a sling, and he bashfully and with trepidation approached the Queen on the steps of Netley Hospital. She pinned the decoration to his serge coat and said some kind words to him. Victoria spent thirty minutes visiting the wards and then she returned to the royal yacht *Alberta* and to Osborne House.

On 14 May 1898, Victoria presented two further Victoria Crosses to wounded soldiers at the hospital. Private Samuel Vickery, Dorset Regiment, and Piper George Findlater, Gordon Highlanders were awarded the decoration for actions in the Tirah Campaign, fought on the North Western Frontier of India between 1897 and 1898. It is worth reproducing an article relating to this visit that was reported in the *St James's Gazette*:

> As usual, her Majesty was in black, though her bonnet had a touch of relief derived from a few white feathers. The Queen, as she stepped from her landau, seemed in wonderful health. Her Highland attendant, Francis Clark, and an Indian attendant helped the

Queen alight. She leaned on his arm on one side, using her stick to support her on the other, and so walked into the entrance-hall of the hospital. Here a wheelchair waited for her, and when she had taken her seat in it the procession moved off to visit the various wards. First the Queen passed through the corridor of the floor given up to the convalescents, these being marshalled in a long row along the corridor. Then she was wheeled to the lift and by it carried up to the third flat – the surgical wards. The great incident here was the presentation of the Victoria Crosses to Piper Findlater, the piper of Dagrai, and to Private Vickery of the Dorset Regiment, who slew several Afridis in stand-up fight, and brought into camp several wounded comrades.

The Royal Victoria Hospital was used during the First World War and treated the poet Wilfred Owen for shell shock before he was transferred to Craiglockhart Hospital in Scotland. It was used during the Second World War to treat the Dunkirk wounded in 1940 and when the US Army took over the facility it served as a hospital for those wounded during D-Day and the Normandy Campaign in 1944. The hospital was closed in 1958 because it was too costly to maintain and the building remained unused for fifteen years until a fire broke out in 1963. During that year demolition work began. All that remains today is the chapel.

Soldiers recuperating from the South African War relaxing on the pier at Netley Hospital, which can be seen in the background. This is the pier that Victoria used during her visits to the hospital. (Wellcome Collection)

72

The Resolute Desk

Victoria presented the Resolute Desk to American President Rutherford B. Hayes.

This double-pedestal partners desk was made from the oak timbers of the Royal Navy Arctic barque HMS *Resolute*. It has been used in the Oval Office in the White House by every American president since Hayes, except for Presidents Johnson, Nixon and Ford during the years 1964 to 1977.

Sir John Franklin led an expedition to search for the Northwest Passage, but he and his entire crew died in 1847. HMS *Resolute* was among several vessels sent to look for Franklin and his crew, but got stuck in the Arctic ice during 1854 and had to be abandoned. The British Government emphasised in *The London Gazette* that *Resolute* remained the property of Her Majesty Queen Victoria, but no attempt was made to send a search and salvage expedition. On 10 September 1855, *Resolute* was located 1,200 miles from the place where she was abandoned by the American whaler *George Henry*, commanded by Captain James Buddington. The United States Government purchased the vessel and paid the costs for its refit before returning it to Britain as a goodwill gesture. United States Navy Commander Henry J. Harstene sailed *Resolute* to England and returned it to Victoria in person on 16 December 1856 at Trinity Pier, East Cowes, Isles of Wight.

Resolute continued to serve with the Royal Navy in home waters until it was retired in 1879. When *Resolute* was broken up, Victoria commissioned three pieces of furniture to be made from her timbers by William Evenden, a cabinetmaker in the joiners' workshop in Chatham Royal Naval Dockyard. A side table was made and retained by the Queen, which is in the Royal Collection. Another desk was given to the wife of Henry Ginnell, the New York merchant and shipowner who funded two expeditions to search for Franklin, which is in the New Bedford Whaling Museum, Massachusetts. Victoria did not forget the generosity of the American Government in renovating and refitting *Resolute* and the third desk was presented to President Hayes as a gesture of thanks in 1880. A brass plaque attached to the desk states:

> HMS *Resolute* forming part of the expedition sent in search of Sir John Franklin in 1852, was abandoned in latitude 74° 41' N. longitude 101° 22' W. on May 15, 1854. She was

discovered and extricated in September 1855 in latitude 67° N. by Captain Buddington of the United States Whaler 'George Henry.' The ship was purchased, fitted out and sent to England as a gift to Her Majesty Queen Victoria by the President and People of the United States as a token of goodwill & friendship. This table was made from her timbers when she was broken up, and is presented by the Queen of Great Britain & Ireland, to the President of the United States as a memorial of the courtesy and loving kindness which dictated the offer of the gift of the '*Resolute*'.

The Resolute Desk was used by the American president in an office on the second floor in the White House in Washington DC. In 1902, the desk remained on the second floor, in a room that would become the president's study, when his office was transferred to the Oval Office in the newly built West Wing. Franklin D. Roosevelt requested that a kneehole be positioned at the rear of the desk to enable him to sit at the desk, while sitting in his wheelchair. He also asked for the door that closed the knee hole be carved with the presidential coat of arms. Roosevelt died in 1945 and did not live to see the renovations made. During the Truman presidency the Resolute Desk was transferred to the broadcast room on the ground floor, which was used by Dwight D. Eisenhower during radio and television broadcasts to the nation. The desk was transferred to the Oval Office at John F. Kennedy's request in 1961. Kennedy's, son John Junior, was photographed peeking through the kneehole as his father reviewed the newspapers in October 1963, a month before Kennedy was assassinated in Dallas, Texas. His successor, Lyndon B. Johnson, used another desk while the Resolute Desk was loaned to the Kennedy Library travelling exhibition during 1964–65 and displayed at the Smithsonian Institute in 1966–77. Jimmy Carter requested the return of the Resolute Desk in January 1977 and it was

President Obama sat at the Resolute Desk in the Oval Office during 2009.

Above: An engraving by George Zobel depicting Victoria's visit to HMS *Resolute*, at Trinity Pier, East Cowes, on the Isle of Wight, on 16 December 1856. (Library of Congress)

Right: A newspaper cutting dated 11 December 1880 that depicts the Resolute Desk. (Library of Congress)

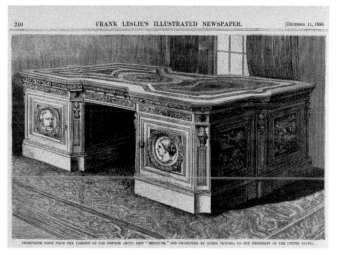

also used by his successor, Ronald Reagan. George Bush preferred to use the desk that he used as vice president when he came to office in 1989, but it was returned to the office in 1993 and used since then by Bill Clinton, George W. Bush, Barack Obama and Donald Trump.

Since Victoria presented the desk to President Hayes in 1880, successive presidents have received gifts from her reign. On 15 February 1964, Prime Minister Harold Wilson presented Lyndon B. Johnson with the ship's bell from HMS *Resolute*.

When Prime Minister Gordon Brown made an official visit to Barack Obama in 2009, he presented the newly elected president with a gift of desk pen holder made from an offcut of timber from Victoria's sloop HMS *Gannet* to compliment the Resolute Desk.

73

Memorial Dedicated to Benjamin Disraeli, Earl of Beaconsfield

Victoria funded a private memorial to be erected on the north side of the chancel of St Michael and All Angels' Church, Hughenden, to commemorate Benjamin Disraeli. It is the only private memorial initiated by a reigning sovereign dedicated to one of her subjects in an English church.

Although he was no longer her Prime Minister, Victoria continued their friendship and they dined together and corresponded through letters. The last time they dined together was on 28 February 1881 at Windsor Castle and she had her final meeting with Disraeli during the following day. On 22 March, Disraeli caught a chill, which developed into bronchitis. Victoria was concerned and when she offered to visit him at Hughenden in March 1881, he declined, because he felt 'she would only ask me to take a message to Albert'.[128] Just before travelling to Osborne House, she wrote a last letter to Disraeli on 5 April 1881. It was accompanied by primroses from Windsor Castle and she promised to send more from Osborne. She wrote: 'You are … constantly in my thoughts and I wish I could do anything to cheer you up.'[129]

Disraeli died on 19 April at his London residence at 19 Curzon Street and his death had a profound effect upon Victoria. She was distraught and the extent of how she valued him as a Prime Minister and as a friend is clearly evident in the words that she wrote in her journal: 'Received the sad news that dear Lord Beaconsfield had passed away. I am most terribly shocked and grieved, for dear Lord Beaconsfield was one of my best, most devoted, and kindest of friends, as well as wisest of counsellors. His loss is irreparable to me and the country. To lose such a power of strength at such a moment is dreadful!'[130]

In the days that followed there was deliberation as to whether he should be buried in Westminster Abbey or at Hughenden. Victoria was involved in discussions with his family. She wrote, 'as regards the funeral, Lord Beaconsfield expresses his wish for it to be private, and that he should be laid near his wife at Hughenden. He was asked, what if the Queen should

---

128. Weintraub, Stanley, *Disraeli, A Biography* (Truman Tally Books, New York, 1993), pp.654–55.

129. Alamy: Queen Victoria's Letter, 5 April 1881.

130. Buckle, Vol. 3. op. cit., p.210.

The memorial dedicated to Benjamin Disraeli funded by Victoria that is located on the north side of the chancel of St Michael and All Angels' Church, Hughenden. (Author's Collection)

wish Westminster Abbey? and he was silent. But I at once said, I did not wish it, but thought that he should be buried at Hughenden as he desired.'[131]

Royal protocol dictated that Victoria could not attend Disraeli's funeral and she sent Bertie, the Prince of Wales, and Prince Leopold to represent her. She sent a wreath comprising primroses with the words 'His favourite flowers, from Osborne, a tribute of affection from Queen Victoria'. On 30 April 1882, four days after he was buried at St Michael and All Angels' Church, Victoria made a private pilgrimage to visit his grave. The flowers from the funeral still remained and she was permitted to look in the vault where Disraeli was laid to rest and to place a wreath of China flowers upon his coffin before it was closed. Victoria then spent some time in Disraeli's home and in particular in his study, where she reflected upon her departed friend.

During the following year, Victoria funded a memorial dedicated to her former Prime Minister and friend, which was unveiled on the day before the first anniversary of her last dinner with Disraeli. It was unprecedented that such a memorial was inaugurated by a reigning monarch to a subject in an English parish church and reveals the closeness of her relationship with him. The inscription on the memorial reads:

> To the dear and honoured memory of Benjamin Earl of Beaconsfield. This memorial is placed by his grateful sovereign and friend Victoria R.I. 'Kings loveth him that speaketh right, February 27th 1882.

---

131. Ibid., p.212.

74

Photograph of Victoria Reading

The year 1882 was an eventful year for Victoria, which included another assassination attempt upon her life.

The year in which this photograph was produced, 1882, marked Victoria's sixty-third birthday and forty-five years as sovereign. On 2 March, Roderick Maclean, a grocer's assistant from Portsmouth, tried to assassinate her as she was being driven in a landau carriage, accompanied by her daughter Princess Beatrice, from Windsor Railway Station to the castle along the High Street. Maclean fired a revolver at her carriage, which was closed with the window down. Before he could fire another shot, he was apprehended by Gordon Wilson, a schoolboy from Eton, who subdued the assailant with an umbrella by striking him over the head and shoulders. Victoria was unaware that someone had tried to kill her until after the event. Maclean's motive was to frighten the Queen and highlight his own poverty and hunger. As he was being taken to the nearest police station for questioning he said: 'I was starving, or I should not have done this.'[132]

The nation was outraged at this attempt upon Victoria's life. During the evening of 2 March, the national anthem was sung at every theatre to show respect and allegiance to the Queen. The news of the assassination attempt was circulated around the world and she received telegrams of sympathy and gratitude from heads of state, including US president Chester Arthur and a message conveyed by the Chinese chargé d'affaires on behalf of the Chinese emperor. On the day after the assassination attempt, Victoria wrote:

I slept as well as usual, and never once thought of what had occurred. Telegrams, as well as letters, pouring in to that extent that I literally spent my whole day opening and reading them. Brown brought the revolver for me to see. It could be fired off in rapid succession with the greatest facility, quite small, but with six chambers. I saw the bullets. Was much relieved to hear that the missing one was found, for it proves that the object was not intimidation, but far worse. God has mercifully protected me! The loyalty manifested on all sides is most touching and gratifying.[133]

---

132. *London Evening Standard*, 4 March 1882.

133. Buckle, Vol. 3. op. cit., p.367.

The image of Victoria reading, a version of which was published in *The Sphere* on 26 January 1901. (Author's Collection)

Touched by the vast numbers of letters and telegrams relating to the assassination attempt, Victoria wrote a letter of thanks to the nation on 12 March 1882, which stated:

> The Queen wishes, before she leaves England, for a short while for some comparative rest and quiet, to express from her heart how very deeply touched she is by the outburst of enthusiastic loyalty, affection and devotion which the painful event of the 2nd instant has called forth from all classes, and from all parts of her vast Empire, as well as by the universal sympathy evinced by the Sovereigns and people of other nations. The Queen cannot sufficiently express how deeply gratified she is by these demonstrations, and would wish to convey to all, from the highest to the humblest, her warmest and most heartfelt thanks. It has ever been her greatest object to do all she can for her subjects, and to uphold the honour and glory of her dear country, as well as to promote the prosperity and happiness of those over whom she has reigned so long, and these efforts will be continued to the last hour of her life. The Queen thanks God that He spared her beloved child, who is her constant and devoted companion, and those who were with her in the moment of danger as well as herself, and she prays that He will continue to protect her for her people's sake as He has hitherto visibly done.[134]

Victoria invited Gordon Wilson to Windsor Castle to personally thank him for his promptitude in stopping Maclean in his assassination attempt. Wilson attained the rank of lieutenant colonel in the army and was killed on 6 November 1914 at Ypres while serving with the Royal Horse Guards.

Maclean had been confined in the Wells Lunatic Asylum and had been released six months before the attempt because he was no longer deemed insane. After his attempt upon Victoria's life, Maclean was tried for high treason at Reading Assizes in April 1882. He was acquitted in the grounds that he was insane and placed in custody at Her Majesty's pleasure. He lived at Broadmoor Lunatic Asylum until his death in 1921.

---

134. *Yorkshire Gazette*, 18 March 1882.

75

John Brown Memorial Bench, Osborne House

On 27 March 1883, Victoria's trusted personal attendant John Brown died at Windsor Castle.

The Memorial Bench erected in memory of John Brown is situated along John Brown Walk, which runs along the eastern side of Osborne House. His head is sculptured on the stone bench with the inscription 'JOHN BROWN 8TH DECEMBER 1826, 27TH MARCH 1883' and a quote from the poet Lord Byron which read 'A TRUE NOBLER TRUSTED HEART. A MORE LOVING AND MORE LOYAL NEVER BEAT WITHIN A HUMAN BREAST.'

Lady Florence Dixie was a regular commentator upon the Irish Question and the Fenian bomb attacks upon public buildings. When she reported that she had been attacked by two men dressed as women at her house in Windsor on 17 March 1883, Victoria sent Brown to her home to appraise the situation and look for any evidence that suggested that she had been attacked. Exposed to the bitterly cold winds that night, he caught a chill while searching Lady Dixie's garden. He returned to Windsor Castle and was ill for the following week and confined to his apartments in Clarence Tower. Brown was suffering from erysipelas and was attended upon by the Queen's physician, Sir William Jenner. His brothers, Archibald and Donald Brown, were also called for, but during his last days he could not recognise anyone.

John, who was aged fifty-seven, died at 11.15 pm on 27 March 1883. When Victoria learnt the news of the death of her favourite servant, whom she had depended upon for nineteen years, she wrote of her sorrow:

> Leopold came to my dressing-room, and broke the dreadful news to me, that my good, faithful Brown, had passed away early this morning. Am terribly upset by this loss, which removes one, who was so devoted and attached to my service and who did so much for my personal comfort. It is the loss not only of a servant, but of a real friend.[135]

---

135. Buckle, Vol. 3. op. cit., p.418.

The John Brown Memorial Bench at Osborne House. (Courtesy of Steve Daniels; www.geograph.org.uk)

The bells at St George's Chapel and the parish church in Windsor were tolled in respect of Brown's passing on the day that he died.

Brown's passing was a tremendous loss to Victoria. In her letter to Lord Cranbrooke two days after he died she wrote, 'that life for the second time is become most trying and sad to bear deprived of all she needs ... the blow has fallen too heavily not to be heavily felt'.[136] Victoria visited his body several times as it lay in Windsor Castle and it was transferred to Balmoral Cemetery for interment.

136. *The Guardian*, 16 December 2004.

76

Postcard of Victoria in her Pony Bath Chair

A bath chair was a light carriage built to accommodate one person with a folding hood that could be opened or closed according to the weather. Mounted on four wheels, they could be pulled by hand or drawn by a pony. Bath chairs were designed to transport disabled persons or individuals with restricted mobility. The name either derived from the fact that they resembled the appearance of a bath tub or they were named after Bath, the town where they were invented by James Heeth around 1750. This particular carriage was made for Victoria in 1893 by R. Bird Cheverton & Company Limited in Newport and donated to the Science Museum by Edward VIII in 1936.

As she entered old age, Victoria became infirm and required assistance in her mobility, especially when travelling across her grounds at Windsor, Balmoral and Osborne. Victoria first mentions using a pony chair on 24 November 1884, when she was aged sixty-six, when she visited the Royal Mausoleum at Frogmore and had to use one to

THE LATE QUEEN VICTORIA.

The postcard of Victoria sitting in the pony bath chair. (Author's Collection)

Victoria is photographed sitting in her pony chair bath with Russian Czar Nicholas II pictured to her immediate left, during a private visit to Balmoral Castle in September 1896. He had been proclaimed as Emperor of Russia four months earlier during May 1896. (Author's Collection)

transport her to the kennels. On 14 April 1886 she mentioned using a pony chair to inspect her garden at Osborne.

Sir Frederick Ponsonby served as Victoria's equerry from 1894. He recalled: 'back at Osborne I found life very peaceful, especially in the winter. The Queen spent July and August there, and also December and January. Her Majesty went out in a pony-chair in the morning accompanied by the Lady-in-Waiting or her Maid of Honour.'[137]

---

137. Ponsonby, op. cit., p.15.

77

Her Majesty's Gracious Smile

Victoria celebrates her Golden Jubilee.

Victoria was frequently depicted as being sombre and in mourning during the latter part of her reign. This unusual photograph of her smiling was captured by Charles Knight and entitled 'Her Majesties Gracious Smile'. It was probably taken during the Aldershot Review in 1887, during her Golden Jubilee year.

Celebrations to commemorate Victoria's Golden Jubilee started early in 1887 in Calcutta when, on 16 February, there was a firework display to celebrate the occasion. The Indian populace enjoyed the spectacle, especially the fireworks when the lines of fire resembled an image of the Queen. However, there was concern in London that the people of England would not be so enthusiastic about the event, because on 14 May Victoria was booed as she was travelling through London from Paddington Station to open the People's Palace in the Mile End Road. Victoria blamed the negative reception upon socialists and the Irish community, who were sympathetic to Irish Home Rule.

The Golden Jubilee, celebrating the fiftieth anniversary of Victoria's accession to the throne, took place on 20 June 1887. Despite pleas from her Prime Minister, Lord Salisbury, to wear ceremonial robes and her crown, Victoria chose to dress in black and wear a bonnet. She was the Head of State of the most powerful Empire in the world, but she would appear the humblest figure in contrast to the fifty sovereigns from Europe and across the world that were invited to Buckingham Palace to celebrate the occasion, who were dressed in their splendid regalia.

Her day began with eating breakfast at Frogmore, before making the journey to Windsor Station, where she boarded the royal train to take her to London. On arrival at Paddington Station she was taken in an open landau to Buckingham Palace. The streets of London were thronged with enthusiastic spectators who cheered her during that journey. Victoria received the invited foreign sovereigns in the picture gallery. A grand luncheon was held in the large dining room, which she had not used since Albert's death in 1861. During the afternoon she received each of her guests in an audience individually and during the evening there was a large banquet. Being Empress of India, Victoria hired two Indian servants, Mohammed Buksh and Abdul Karim. Karim would become Victoria's teacher, secretary and close friend during the final years of her reign.

The postcard depicting the smiling Victoria. (Library of Congress)

The Golden Jubilee celebrations continued the following day with a service of thanksgiving at Westminster Abbey. Victoria rode in an open landau escorted by Colonial Indian Cavalry and was cheered along the route. After the thanksgiving service, Victoria returned to Buckingham Palace where she greeted the crowds from the balcony. Although the large crowds demonstrated the popularity of the monarchy, she reigned over a divided nation, where there was dissension regarding the problems with Ireland and there was a large division between the rich and the poor.

Victoria was indeed overwhelmed by the reception that she received during the Golden Jubilee celebrations.

In her diary on 20 June 1887, she wrote, 'Fifty years today since I came to the throne. God has mercifully sustained me through many great trials and sorrows.'[138]

---

138. Royal Archives: RA VIC/MAIN/QVJ (W), 20 June 1887. (Courtesy HM Queen Elizabeth II).

78

HMS *Gannet*

Victoria's sloop HMS *Gannet* participated in the siege of Suakin in Sudan during September to October 1888.

Laid down on the River Medway at the Royal Dockyard, Sheerness, in 1877 and launched on 31 August 1878, HMS *Gannet* is an example of a sloop of Victoria's Royal Navy. Her purpose was to protect the British Empire and its trade routes. The hull was constructed from teak planking on an iron frame. Its complement comprised 139 crew, and, powered by steam and sail, it could travel at a speed of 15 knots. Armed with three 64-pounder guns, *Gannet* was a major instrument deployed in gunboat diplomacy and was used in that role in 1888 during the siege of Suakin.

Commissioned in April 1879, *Gannet* was deployed in the Pacific until 1883, patrolling the seas and protecting British interests in the region. In July 1883 she returned to Sheerness, where she underwent a two-year refit. *Gannet* was then deployed to the Mediterranean Fleet, where she supported British land forces commanded by Major-General Sir Gerald Graham during the Suakin Expedition in the Sudan. Part of her role was to stop and search ships in anti-slave trade operations.

Gannet was being refitted in Malta when her commander received orders on 11 September 1888, to relieve HMS *Dolphin* at the besieged port of Suakin, Sudan. On 17 September she engaged anti-Anglo-Egyptian forces led by Osman Digna, a self-proclaimed Mahdi. It was reported in the *Penny Illustrated*:

HMS *Gannet* has also proved galling to the enemy attacking Souakim [sic Suakin]. This Red Sea port has been greatly harassed from the land side. During Thursday night, Sept. 27, 'the Rebels' entrenched themselves in new positions, one being 500 yards in front of the left water fort, and another 800 yards to the left of that fort. Until midnight a heavy fire was continued on both sides – the *Gannet* using her machine guns, as well as her cannon. Deserters from the right trenches report that the enemy suffered severely, one of the shells killing seventeen men, and another nine. The casualties on our side were three wounded, in the right water fort. The telephone wire connecting the forts with the town was again cut during the night. Owing to the heavy fire from the *Gannet* and

HMS *Gannet* moored at Chatham Historic Dockyard in Kent. (Author's Collection)

the forts the rebels were on Sunday forced to withdraw, with considerable loss, from the trenches cut 500 yards in front of the water fort.[139]

Gannet took part in the siege of this port for nearly a month, firing two hundred main armament shells and nearly 1,200 Nordenfelt rounds. *Gannet* was relieved by HMS *Starling* on 15 October and paid off at Malta on 1 November 1888. *Gannet* spent the following seven years surveying the Mediterranean before returning to Sheerness, where she was decommissioned. *Gannet* is on display at Chatham Historic Dockyard.

---

139. *The Penny Illustrated*, 6 October 1888.

79

Mourning Dress Worn by Victoria in 1894

It was traditional for women living in the Victorian era to wear mourning dress for a year following the death of a spouse. Thirty-three years after the death of Albert, Victoria still continued to wear mourning dress such as this example, which is made of silk. Victoria insisted that all her family and household staff wore black armbands for eight years after the prince's death. Queen Victoria also suffered the loss of two children, Princess Alice and Prince Leopold, and one grandchild, Princess May. During the 1890s she would suffer further family bereavements.

Victoria's grandchild Prince Albert Victor died of influenza at Sandringham on 14 January 1892, a few weeks before his wedding. He was aged twenty-eight and was the eldest son of Edward, Prince of Wales, which meant that the young prince was second in line of succession. He led a controversial life, accused of being homosexual and of leading a promiscuous lifestyle. It was rumoured, but never substantiated, that he patronised a male brothel in Cleveland Street, London, and was also suspected of being Jack the Ripper, who murdered five women between 1888 and 1891.

The news of Prince Albert Victor's demise caused further distress to Victoria as she suffered another bereavement within her family. Six months before her own death, Victoria would lose another child when her son Alfred died from throat cancer on 30 July 1900. It was an awful shock, because she was unaware that he had been battling the disease.

This black dress was typical of the traditional mourning attire that she wore for the last forty years of her reign and shows how her physique had change from the slim and slender frame to a large, stout figure. Victoria set a trend and it was expected that the bereaved would wear black for a period of mourning that would last between three months to two and a half years in respect for a departed loved one. The poor, who could not afford a change of clothing, would dye their clothes black. The amount of black worn was determined by the various stages of mourning. A completely black dress signified full mourning, but small amounts of white were permitted to be worn for half mourning. The subtle white trim around the sleeves and neckline together with the subtle use of crinkled crepe on this dress signifies a state of half mourning. Lighter material was used for the bodice to enable comfort during warm summer months.

Victoria's black mourning dress, which is on display at the Brooklyn Museum Costume Collection at the Metropolitan Museum of Art in New York. It was a gift of the Brooklyn Museum in 2009, this institution having, in turn, received it as a gift from a private collector, C.W. Howard, in 1950. Victoria sold her clothes every year and a collector friend of C.W. Howard obtained this item in London immediately after the Diamond Jubilee in 1897. (Courtesy of the Metropolitan Museum of Art, New York)

80

Four Sovereigns Commemorative Medallion

On 23 June 1894, Edward, the eldest child of the Duke of York, who was Victoria's great grandson, was born. Three years later a medallion was produced to commemorate the unprecedented situation where Victoria and three successive heirs were living in the same period.

On 16 July 1894, Victoria travelled by train from Windsor to Richmond to attend the christening of her great grandson, Edward, Duke of York, at the royal residence, White Lodge, Richmond Park. The ceremony was conducted by Edward Benson, Archbishop of Canterbury. The baby wore the old Honiton Lace Robe, which was made for the christening of Vicky, the Princess Royal, and was worn by all her children and English grandchildren at their christenings. He was christened Edward Albert Christian George Andrew Patrick David; the last four names being the Patron Saints of England, Scotland, Ireland and Wales.

Several photographs were taken of Victoria and her three heirs. This one was taken at Osborne House on 5 August 1899 during her eightieth year and features, from left to right:

The front and rear of the commemorative four sovereigns medallion. (Author's Collection)

FOUR GENERATIONS of BRITISH SOVEREIGNS. BEAGLES POSTCARDS.
THEIR LATE MAJESTIES QUEEN VICTORIA. KING EDWARD VII. AND KING GEORGE V;
HIS MAJESTY KING EDWARD VIII. WHEN A CHILD.

A postcard with the four current or future sovereigns pictured together. (Author's Collection)

Prince George, Duke of York, later, George V; Queen Victoria; Edward, Prince of Wales, later Edward VII; and Edward, Prince of York, later Edward VIII, who became Duke of Windsor after his abdication in 1936 when he married American divorcee Wallis Simpson. Victoria realised the significance of this important photograph, which shows four British sovereigns, and commented that 'it seems that it has never happened in this Country that there should be three direct Heirs as well as the Sovereign alive'.[140]

It would take a further 119 years until there were again living heirs to the throne, when in 2013 Catherine, Duchess of Cambridge, gave birth to Prince George, son of William, Duke of Cambridge, grandson of Charles, Prince of Wales, and great-grandson of Queen Elizabeth II.

---

140. National Portrait Gallery website.

81

Abdul Karim, 'The Munshi'

Abdul Karim became Victoria's Indian secretary during 1894.

Abdul Karim and Mohammed Buksh were two Indian nationals who were employed to serve dinner at Buckingham Palace for her Golden Jubilee celebration dinner. They both kissed Victoria's feet when they met her for the first time. Buksh served for sixteen years as servant to General Thomas Dennehy, who was a British representative in Rajputna. Karim was employed as a clerk to the governor of Agra jail (close to where the Taj Mahal, one of the wonders of the world, was built) and he believed that he was to be riding on horseback as an escort for the Queen. Instead his role was as a junior footman, waiting tables on 20 June 1887, the day of the Golden Jubilee celebrations. Karim would become a prominent person in Victoria's life, breaking through the walls of racial and class prejudice within the court to become a friend. In 1888, he was proclaimed 'the Munshi' (translated as 'the teacher') to Victoria. In 1894, he became her Indian Secretary.

Victoria was enamoured by the presence of her Indian servants, in particular Abdul Karim, aged twenty-four, who was the son of an Agra doctor. Although they were employed temporarily for the Golden Jubilee, she enjoyed their company. On the following day, 29 June, Victoria received foreign dignitaries at a garden party at Buckingham Palace where Karim and Buksh were present as escorts and stood outside her tent. The next day the Queen received a delegation of Indian princes in the drawing room at Windsor Castle. Karim and Buksh were in attendance.

Wherever Victoria went, her two Indian servants followed. During August 1887, Karim began teaching the Empress of India Hindustani. She confirmed: 'Am learning a few words of Hindustani, to speak to my servants. It is a great interest to me, for both the language and the people, I have naturally never come into real contact with, before.'[141] Towards the end August 1887, she wrote: 'The one Abdul is beginning to teach me a little Hindustani which interests me and amuses me very much.'[142]

---

141. Royal Archives: RA VIC/MAIN/QVJ (W), 3 August 1887. (Courtesy HM Queen Elizabeth II).

142. Royal Archives: RA VIC/MAIN/QVJ (W), 30 August 1887. (Courtesy HM Queen Elizabeth II).

Victoria and Abdul Karim.
(Author's Collection)

Karim very rapidly became a permanent member of the Queen's household and would become a favourite, a confidante and someone she could depend upon. With Victoria enchanted by his personality and charm, Karim would fill the vacuum in her life that was left by Albert and John Brown. He also taught her aspects of Indian culture during daily lessons, and she was able to write her journal in Urdu. Karim became known as the Munshi and Victoria soon began to revaluate Karim's role for she recognised that it was a mistake to bring him from India just to wait at tables. It was something that he had never done, given that he was a clerk. He was anxious to return home because he was unhappy with the situation. The Queen valued his intelligence and companionship. She was also intent on learning Hindustani, given that she was Empress of India. During 1888, Victoria was making efforts to elevate Karim's position within her court.

They would become close friends and Victoria commissioned a portrait to be painted of him. In 1894, she promoted Karim as her Indian Secretary and gave him the title 'Hafiz'. The role was not a political position, but to assist the Queen with her correspondence. He was rewarded with a property at Windsor and cottages on her estates at Osborne and Balmoral.

The relationship between Victoria and the Munshi antagonised and caused concern among her family, politicians and courtiers, who were not enamoured by their friendship. Karim was Muslim, with dark skin, and the British establishment, with their bigoted aloofness and inherent racial and religious prejudice, felt threatened by his presence. Bertie, Prince of Wales and Dr Sir James Reid, the Queen's physician, greatly despised Karim and the influence he had upon the sovereign. Victoria's determination to continue her friendship with Karim demonstrated that she abhorred racial and religious intolerance, was keen to broaden her horizons and craved intimacy. After Albert, Victoria had close relationships with men that were deemed outsiders. Benjamin Disraeli, John Brown and Abdul Karim had risen from the lower echelons of society, regarded by the people who surrounded Victoria with scepticism, but had succeeded in charming the widowed monarch. After the death of Victoria in 1901, Karim was ordered out of his home and returned to India with a pension. His personal papers, which contained details of his relationship with the Queen, were burned. Karim died in 1909 aged forty-six.

82

The Longest Reign in History Brooch

On 23 September 1896, Victoria surpassed the reign of George III as longest-serving British monarch.

Victoria, who was then aged seventy-eight, became the longest-serving British monarch on 23 September 1896, exceeding the reign of her grandfather, King George III, who ruled for fifty-nine years, three months and four days, and several other long-reigning British sovereigns that included James VI of Scotland and I of England, fifty-seven years; Henry III, fifty-six years; Edward III, fifty years; and Elizabeth I, forty-four years.

I t was a remarkable achievement for Victoria to have reigned for six decades. Despite receiving congratulations from across the nation, there existed a strong appetite to commemorate this landmark, but Victoria insisted that celebrations should be deferred until 1897, the

The front and rear of a brooch produced to mark Victoria's achievement in becoming the longest-reigning monarch at that time. (Author's Collection)

sixtieth anniversary of her ascension to the throne. On 20 June 1897, Victoria had reigned for sixty years and she was the first British sovereign to celebrate her Diamond Jubilee. It was also the first time that the term diamond had been used in relation to commemoration of a sixtieth anniversary in the history of the British monarchy. Several other sovereigns around the world have reigned for six decades.

Victoria had outlived all the members who attended her first Privy Council in 1837 and all her nine bridesmaids who were in attendance at her wedding. During the course of her reign, she was served by ten Prime Ministers and five Archbishops of Canterbury. There were also eighteen presidents of the United States of America and she had seen France ruled by one king, one emperor and seven presidents of the Republic.

When Victoria died in 1901, she held the record for the longest-reigning British sovereign after sixty-three years on the throne. That distinction was surpassed in 2015 by Elizabeth II, who is currently in her seventieth year as a serving monarch.

83

Victoria's Diamond Jubilee Medal

The Diamond Jubilee Medal was a decoration awarded to members of the royal family, the court, dignitaries and guests who attended the celebrations, and selected servicemen who formed the jubilee parade in London. The Diamond Jubilee of Queen Victoria was celebrated on 22 June 1897, two days after she reached her sixtieth year as Britain's sovereign, and involved a royal procession comprising seventeen carriages through the streets of London to St Paul's Cathedral, where a thanksgiving service was held, before she returned to Buckingham Palace. The procession was not only a commemoration of Britain's longest-serving sovereign, but a celebration of the British Empire.

Victoria's Diamond Jubilee was a lavish affair, a spectacular pageant that was representative of the Empire. The heads of European states, many of which were related to the British monarchy, alongside the prime ministers representing all colonies within the British Empire, gave the nation another opportunity to posture and assert itself on the world stage, as well as celebrate past achievements, a strong economy, innovations in technology and victories in the numerous wars fought during her reign.

To commemorate the event, the Diamond Jubilee Medal was instituted as a decoration that was awarded to those involved with the official celebrations including the royal family, members of the royal household, government officials, foreign envoys, colonial prime ministers and selected members of the armed services. There were three different versions of the medal: the Queen's Jubilee Diamond Medal, which was produced in a further three variations, in gold, silver and bronze. Seventy-three gold medals were awarded to members of the royal family, 3,040 silver medals were issued to officers and 890 bronze medals were given to other ranks. An image of Victoria wearing a veil is shown on the front of the medal, while on the reverse are the words 'IN COMMEMORATION OF THE 60TH YEAR OF THE REIGN OF QUEEN VICTORIA, 20 JUNE 1897', enclosed within a garland of roses, thistles and shamrocks.

A diamond-shaped medal was awarded to mayors and provosts who took part in the celebrations. Fourteen gold medals were presented to lord mayors and lord provosts and 512 silver medals of similar design were awarded to mayors and provosts across the United Kingdom. A special Police Diamond Jubilee Medal was awarded to 10,086 police officers who were on duty on the day of the celebrations.

Above left and above right: The front and reverse of Queen Victoria's Diamond Jubilee Medal in silver. The silver version was awarded to officers and those of similar status, a total of 3,040 being presented.

Right: A special diamond-shaped Jubilee Medal was produced for mayors and provosts across the United Kingdom. Examples in gold were presented to lord mayors and lord provosts (fourteen in total), whilst 512 silver variants were given to mayors and provosts.

An official photograph released to mark Victoria's diamond jubilee. This picture was actually taken on 6 July 1893 when Victoria attended the wedding of her grandson, the future King George V, to Princess Mary of Teck. She is seen wearing the lace worn at her own wedding, her wedding veil surmounted by the Small Diamond Crown. (Author's Collection)

84

Diamond Jubilee Inscription at St Paul's Cathedral

Victoria's Diamond Jubilee procession paused briefly by the steps of the western entrance of St Paul's Cathedral, which had been transformed into an amphitheatre. A brief open-air service took place in order to ensure that the frail sovereign, aged seventy-eight and suffering from painful arthritis, did not have to leave the carriage to climb the steps to enter the cathedral. An inscription denotes the spot where Victoria's carriage stopped briefly on 22 June 1897.

The service of thanksgiving on the steps of St Paul's Cathedral lasted for twenty minutes, during which time the Queen remained in her carriage. A large choir and orchestra were assembled to greet Victoria, alongside members of the clergy and dignitaries. The service consisted of a performance of *Ta Deum*, followed by prayers, a benediction and concluded with the hymn *Old Hundredth*.

Although Victoria was impressed by the service, her cousin, Augusta, Grand Duchess of Mecklenburg-Strelitz, was appalled that, after reigning for sixty years, she should 'thank God in the street'.

The inscription at the foot of the steps leading to the western entrance of St Paul's Cathedral is on the exact spot where Victoria's carriage stopped for the service of thanksgiving. (Author's Collection)

Andrew Carrick Gow's depiction of Victoria arriving for the Diamond Jubilee service on 22 June 1897. (Guildhall Art Gallery)

It was reported in the *Morning Post*:

The ceremony at St Paul's was perhaps the most impressive and contemporary London has seen. The great choirs were admirably arranged, the music was beautiful, and the chants and responses resounded clearly far beyond the immediate precinct within which the Thanksgiving Service could be seen and heard. When at the close the first notes of the '*Old Hundredth*' were raised the whole great assembly, that filled the amphitheatre round the west end of the Cathedral place joined in the familiar hymn with an effect that could not but touch all those who were so placed as to hear the swelling chorus. This was followed by the National Anthem, and then by three cheers for the Queen, perhaps the most impressive ever heard in time of peace. As the Queen drove away she was deeply moved.[143]

The Queen was once again overwhelmed by the reception that she received for she wrote:

In weal and woe I have ever had the true sympathy of all my people, which has been warmly reciprocated by myself. It has given me unbounded pleasure to see so many of my subjects from all parts of the world assembled here, and to find them joining in the acclamations of loyal devotion to myself, and I wish to thank them all from the depth of my grateful heart.[144]

143. *Morning Post*, 23 June 1897.

144. Browne, op. cit., pp.157–8.

85

Menu for the Spithead Diamond Jubilee Review

The Royal Navy paid homage to honour Victoria's sixty-year reign at the Spithead Review on 26 June 1897. A lunch was given on aboard the Cunard Royal Mail steamship *Campania* in honour of the event. Seventeen royal reviews of the fleet took place at Spithead during Victoria's reign. The first took place in 1842 and the last was held during 1899. At 8 am on 22 June 1897, a sixty-gun salute was fired to mark each year of the Queen's reign. HMS *Victory*, flying the Royal Standard alongside the Admiral's flag, fired the first shot.

Victoria was too frail to attend the Diamond Jubilee Review on 26 June 1897 in person and she was represented by the Prince of Wales in reviewing the fleet that was anchored in the Solent. The review involved 165 vessels from Victoria's Royal Navy, including twenty-one British battleships and fifty-six cruisers in addition to smaller craft, manned by 38,600 personnel. The British contingent formed only a part of the Royal Navy, for the majority were deployed across the British Empire. Twelve foreign navies sent representatives to participate in the review at Spithead, including the Russian Cruiser *Rossiya*, the American cruiser *Brooklyn* and the French cruiser *Pothuan*. This vast assemblage of naval power was anchored in seven lines from Stokes Bay east towards Horse Sands Fort. Sixty of those vessels had fired a salute for the sovereign four days earlier while the celebrations were taking place in London.

The Prince of Wales inspected each vessel anchored in the review in the royal yacht *Victoria and Albert II*. Each ship played 'God save the Queen', and the officers and men gave three cheers for the prince as it passed. Each ship fired a salute of ten guns.

During that evening, the prince embarked aboard the royal yacht *Alberta* to view the fleet, which was illuminated at night from 9.15 pm until midnight.

The review was an opportunity to show the strength of Victoria's Royal Navy, to confirm its supremacy as a sea power and to highlight its importance as an instrument with which to protect the British Empire. It demonstrated the growth of modern sea power. Throughout Victoria's sixty-year reign it had transformed from the obsolete wooden walls of the age of Nelson into a larger, stronger force with ironclads that were larger and faster, with formidable firepower.

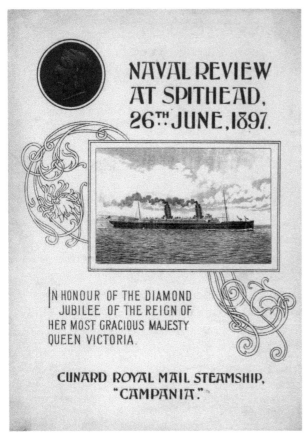

NAVAL REVIEW AT SPITHEAD, 26ᵀᴴ JUNE, 1897.

IN HONOUR OF THE DIAMOND JUBILEE OF THE REIGN OF HER MOST GRACIOUS MAJESTY QUEEN VICTORIA.

CUNARD ROYAL MAIL STEAMSHIP, "CAMPANIA."

Left: A lunch menu for those on board the steamship *Campania* during the Spithead Diamond Jubilee Review. (New York Public Library)

Below: This painting by Charles Dixon was entitled *In honour of our Queen – Queen Victoria's Diamond Jubilee at Spithead*. The Royal Yacht *Victoria and Albert II*, carrying the Prince of Wales, is pictured in the foreground on the right, flying the Royal Standard. HMS *Renown* is pictured on the immediate left, leading the long line of Majestic-class battleships. In the distance, behind the Royal Yacht *Victoria and Albert II*, can be seen, on the right, the Russian cruiser *Rossiya* and the white-hulled US Navy cruiser *Brooklyn*. (Royal Museums Greenwich)

86

Map of the British Empire

Victoria was the most powerful woman in the world.

By 1897, the year of her Diamond Jubilee, Victoria reigned over a British Empire of approximately 400 million people, amounting to nearly a quarter of the world's population.

The Battle of Waterloo in 1815, brought an end to the seventeen-year war with France and heralded a period of peace in Europe (with the exception of the Crimean War) that would last for ninety-nine years until the beginning of the First World War, a period that was known as Pax Britannica. Victoria inherited the British Empire when she ascended the throne. Canada had been captured from the French after the Seven Years' War in 1763 and Britain was able to trade its resources of timber, furs and ores. British settlers established a colony at the Cape of Good Hope in South Africa during the early part of the nineteenth century. The port provided an ideal stopping point for British ships transporting merchant goods between Britain and South Africa and the Empire was able to utilise its opulent diamond and gold resources. Australia had become a penal colony during the end of the eighteenth century and was a British colony by the time of Victoria's accession.

Victoria would become the ruler of the largest empire in history due to the Royal Navy's supremacy of the seas, which enabled Britain to defend its colonies and protect trade routes. Britain had enhanced the use of steam, increased production of coal and iron and undergone an industrial revolution that enabled the country to produce low-cost goods that could be exported internationally, strengthening the British economy.

During Victoria's reign, the British Empire would flourish and expand in the Asian, African, Australasian, North and South American continents. The desire to spread democracy and Christianity to improve lives was a motivation to expand, although conquered countries regarded it as oppression and recognised that the underlying motive was greed. The French, Spanish, Dutch and Ottoman Empires were in decline and Britain exploited their weakened positions to take advantage and expand without being challenged. Victoria's long reign brought stability and she became the symbol of a vast and strong empire.

The First Colonial Conference was held in London between 4 April and 6 May 1887, when representatives from the colonies within the British Empire attended the Queen's Diamond Jubilee. Hosted by Victoria and her Prime Minister, Lord Salisbury, its purpose was to foster

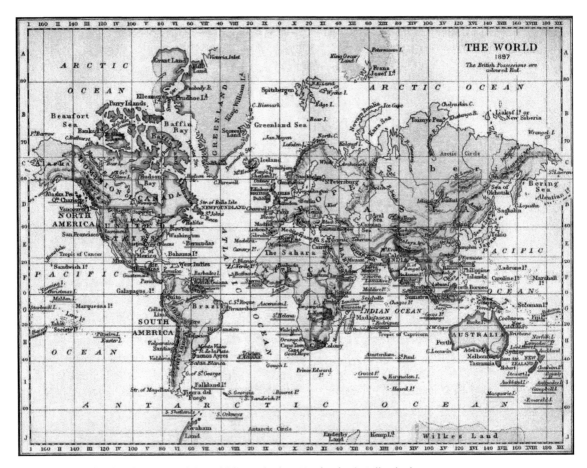

A map showing the extent of the British Empire in 1897. (Author's Collection)

closer ties between Britain and her colonies. The agenda mainly focused upon defence of the Empire, but it was agreed that Australia would pay Britain £126,000 annually for the Royal Navy to maintain a presence in the Pacific, that a telegraph cable would be financed to link Vancouver and Australia, and to ratify that the sovereign's title should be extended to 'Queen of the United Kingdom of Great Britain, Ireland and the Colonies, and all Dependencies thereof, and Empress of India'. Further Colonial Conferences were convened in 1894, 1897 and 1902, and after the First World War they would be known as Imperial Conferences. In 1936 these meetings were renamed a 'Commonwealth of Nations', which was the beginning of the transition from Empire into Commonwealth. The British Empire declined after the Second World War, but many of the countries that were once colonies maintained links with Britain through the Commonwealth after they had gained their independence.

87

Foundation Stone of Victoria and Albert Museum

Victoria laid this foundation stone at the Victoria and Albert Museum.

It was Prince Albert's ambition that a museum should be built on a site south of Hyde Park, specifically devoted to science and art. Funded from the remaining proceeds of the Great Exhibition, the Victoria and Albert Museum was initially inaugurated as a decorative art museum in 1852. It was known as the Museum of Manufacture and its intention was to make art accessible to everyone. It was officially opened at Marlborough House before it was transferred to its current location on the Cromwell Road in 1857, and it was known as the South Kensington Museum. During 1899, work began on completing the building of the museum and Victoria was asked to lay the foundation stone.

On 17 May 1899, Victoria travelled in an open state landau carriage from Buckingham Palace to the junction of Cromwell Road and Exhibition Road, where she laid the foundation stone for what would become the grand entrance to the museum. It would be known as the Victoria and Albert Museum in honour and acknowledgement of Prince Albert's enthusiasm for the project. During that morning she learned that Lord Strafford, a former page and groom who later served as an equerry, had been killed in a tragic train accident when he fell onto the track at Potters Bar Station in front of a passing Great Northern express train. Despite this sad news, Victoria carried on with the engagement to lay the stone and formally sanction the new name of the museum. The ceremony was scheduled to take place at 4.15 pm and an enormous marquee was erected that could accommodate 2,500 guests. Victoria arrived heralded by a fanfare of trumpets and students from the Royal College of Music sang the National Anthem as she remained in her carriage.

Victoria's address at the ceremony was published in full in *The Times*:

It is a great pleasure to me to be here to lay the foundation-stone of the building which will worthily contain the magnificent collection of objects illustrating the fine and industrial arts which have been brought together on this site during the period of my reign. My interest in this great institution which in its inception and during its early

Above: The foundation stone laid down by Victoria on her last official public engagement. (Author's Collection)

Below left and below right: The entrance to the Victoria and Albert Museum showing the sculptures of Victoria and Albert above the doorway and the foundation stone left in the photo. (Author's Collection)

days I shared with my dear husband has grown with its progress and development; and I rejoice that I have been able to take a personal part in the completion of a scheme which will be not the least distinction of my reign, and which will, I trust, continue to be a powerful factor in the industrial enlightenment and artistic training of my people. I am pleased that the priceless collection of treasures which the munificence of private persons and the public spirit of Parliament have brought together will always be associated with my name and my dear husband's. In compliance with your prayer, I gladly direct that in future, the institution should be styled the 'Victoria and Albert Museum'; and I trust that it will remain for ages a monument of discerning liberality and a source of refinement and progress.[145]

The Queen was handed some coins that featured the present year's date and they were placed in a casket, which was locked by the Prince of Wales with a golden key that was retained by Her Majesty. The casket was then placed in a cavity in the foundation stone. A mallet was then passed to the Queen for the purpose of laying the stone. The cement was spread by Victoria, the Prince of Wales, the Lord President of the Council and the architect Aston Webb. The foundation stone was then laid upon the cement, the Queen tapped the stone with the mallet and then passed it to Webb. The Prince of Wales then proclaimed 'In the name of Her Majesty the Queen, I declare this stone well and truly laid.'

The foundation stone was originally laid by Victoria at the junction on Cromwell Road and Exhibition Road, but it was incorporated into the design of the entrance to the museum. Webb designed the façade of the Victoria and Albert Museum, which comprised a cupola and featured sculptures of Victoria and Albert immediately above the entrance. This section of the building was not completed until 1909, when it was opened to the public. The foundation stone can be seen at the museum entrance. It reads:

THIS STONE WAS LAID BY HER MAJESTY QUEEN VICTORIA
EMPRESS OF INDIA, ON THE 17TH DAY OF MAY 1899, IN THE
62ND YEAR OF HER REIGN, FOR THE COMPLETION OF THE
SOUTH KENSINGTON MUSEUM, INAUGERATED BY HIS
ROYAL HIGHNESS, THE PRINCE CONSORT, AND HENCEFORTH
TO BE KNOWN AS THE VICTORIA AND ALBERT MUSEUM.

---

145. *The Times*, 18 May 1899.

88

Portrait of Victoria

Baron Heinrich von Angeli painted this portrait during 1899.

Victoria had sat for Baron Heinrich von Angeli for two portraits at Windsor Castle in 1885. The Austrian artist was favoured by the Queen, who enjoyed his sense of humour, commenting that 'he is aged and less lively, but otherwise as amusing as ever'.[146] Fourteen years later, Baron von Angeli returned to Windsor Castle to paint another portrait of the Queen. He began this portrait on 18 May 1899 and continued on 19 and 22 May. By 25 May Angeli had made sufficient progress for Victoria to comment: 'After luncheon I sat again for some time to Angeli, who is making an admirable picture.'[147] Princess Beatrice read to Victoria as von Angeli painted her at each session. After a further sitting on 3 July she described the portrait as 'wonderfully good and nearly finished'.[148] Baron von Angeli completed the portrait on 12 July 1899 and the Queen informed the Empress Frederick that it was the 'best and likest he ever painted of me'.

Despite her ailments and frailty, the Queen had a busy year during the year that this portrait was painted. She spent March to April in the French Riviera and on 15 May she visited Kensington Palace, her birthplace, before the state rooms and the banqueting room were opened to the public. This was her last visit to the palace and she had to be carried up the state staircase. Although she spent the first nineteen years of her life in Kensington Palace, Victoria commented in her journal that it was the first time that she had visited George, Prince of Denmark's, accommodation in the Denmark Wing during this final visit.

On 29 September, she presented colours to the 2nd Battalion, Seaforth Highlanders, on the lawn in front of Balmoral. Two weeks later, on 12 October, Britain took up arms once again with the beginning of the South African War.

---

146. Royal Archives: RA VIC/MAIN/QVJ (W), 3 March 1885. (Courtesy HM Queen Elizabeth II).

147. Royal Archives: RA VIC/MAIN/QVJ (W), 25 May 1899. (Courtesy HM Queen Elizabeth II).

148. Royal Archives: RA VIC/MAIN/QVJ (W), 25 May 1899. (Courtesy HM Queen Elizabeth II).

The portrait of Victoria by Baron Heinrich von Angeli. (Author's Collection)

89

The Queen's South Africa Medal

The South African War, also known as the Second Anglo-Boer War, was fought between 11 October 1899 and 31 May 1902.

South Africa's resources such as diamonds and gold attracted British colonists. This caused conflict with Boer states that wanted to protect their territory and assets. Boer guerrillas attacked British forces stationed in the colony on 1 October 1899 and war was officially declared ten days later. Five hundred thousand British soldiers, together with contingents from the Empire, were sent to South Africa to fight eighty-eight thousand soldiers belonging to the two Boer states, the South African Republic (Transvaal) and the Orange Free State. This is the Queen's South Africa War campaign medal, which was issued to soldiers who fought the South African War.

The South African War had a direct impact upon Victoria, because her nephew, Major Count Gleichen, 3rd Battalion, Grenadier Guards, was wounded in the neck during the early part of the conflict. Also, the actions of the British Army during the war, in particular the establishment of concentration camps in South Africa, tarnished the reputation of the Empire during the final years of her reign. The wives and children of Boer guerrilla fighters were sent to these concentration camps between 1900 and 1902, where 26,000 died from disease and starvation. It is believed that concern for the impact of the South African War upon the Empire exacerbated the Queen's declining health.

Soldiers from the Empire, including Australia, Canada, India and New Zealand, fought alongside the British Army and experienced difficulty in fighting the Boer guerrillas, who were highly competent, skilled horseman and marksmen. They also had to fight with limited resources and food, and had to contend with disease. The Boer resistance eventually disintegrated in 1902, a year after Victoria's death.

Designs for the Queen's South Africa Medal were submitted to Victoria for her approval by March 1899. The British Army, Royal Navy, colonial forces, local allied South African units, informants and war correspondents who served in South Africa from 11 October 1899 until 31 May 1902 were eligible for the decoration. Approximately 178.000 received the medal.

This particular Queen's South Africa Medal was awarded to the author's great grandfather, Private William David Evans, who served with the 2nd Lincolnshire Regiment. The crowned

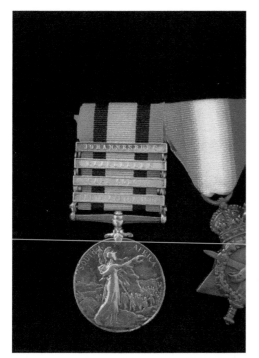

Above left and above right: The front and rear of the Queen's South Africa Medal. (Author's Collection)

and veiled head of Victoria and the words 'VICTORIA REGINA ET IMPERATRIX' are inscribed around the edge on the front of the medal. The reverse of the medal depicts Britannia with a flag in her left hand holding out a laurel wreath towards an advancing party of soldiers. Two warships can be seen in the rear. The wreath in Britannia's hand points to the letter 'R' in the word 'AFRICA', which is inscribed around the rim. The following clasps are attached to it: 'Paardeberg', 'Johannesberg', 'Cape Colony' and 'South Africa 1901'.

90

Victoria's Chocolate Box Gift

Towards the end of 1899, Victoria sent a chocolate box to every British soldier and officer who participated in the South African War as a gift.

The chocolate boxes were made of tin and had rounded images, and they were designed to be portable for easy storage in a soldier's kit bag or pocket. Each box was attractively decorated with a boldly embossed medallion image of Her Majesty, alongside her Cipher 'VR', denoting 'Victoria Regina'. The words 'South Africa 1900' and in Victoria's handwriting 'I wish you a Happy New Year', are inscribed on the tin.

Victoria commissioned three chocolate manufacturers, S. Fry & Sons, Rowntree & Company Ltd and Cadbury Brothers Ltd, to supply the chocolate. These companies were owned by families who were Quakers. They refused to profit from the war and donated the chocolate to be sent to troops serving in South Africa.

Funding for the production costs was personally financed from the Queen's purse. Barclay & Fry Ltd were appointed designers, but each of the three chocolate manufacturers commissioned different companies to provide the tins, which meant there were three types of boxes with different dimensions and colouring. When the chocolate had been consumed, the box could be retained as a memento from the war. The gold-embossed image of the Queen was detachable and could be used as a medal.

The Queen's present of chocolate boxes attracted much attention from the media and the public before they were distributed to the troops in South Africa. It was feared that entrepreneurs would imitate the boxes for commercial gain and reduce the significance of this special, unique and unprecedented gift from sovereign to soldier, to the extent that the following notice was published in *The Times*:

> In view of the national interest taken in Her Majesty's New Year present to her soldiers in South Africa and Her Majesty's desire that no other boxes should be made like those presented, and as illustrations of these boxes have appeared in some of the daily or other newspapers, we are authorised to ask if you will give publicity to the fact that these royal

An example of the chocolate box gifted by Victoria to soldiers serving in South Africa on New Year's Day 1900. (Author's Collection)

chocolate boxes, have, under royal authority, been duly registered and otherwise protected in every way ... in order to prevent imitations of these boxes.[149]

Sir Francis Evans MP, chairman of Union Steamship Company, offered on behalf of the company to transport the chocolate from Britain to South Africa free of charge, which was accepted by the Secretary of State for War. The first consignment was transported by the *Mexican* from Southampton on 16 December 1899.

A total of 123,000 tins were produced, each containing half a pound of vanilla chocolate, in four layers, and they were sent to soldiers serving in South Africa in time for the New Year. An Army Order, issued in April 1900, authorised that the tins could be forwarded to wounded soldiers who had been invalided home before the arrival of the Queen's present, and to the next of kin of fallen soldiers. The gift was well received and valued by the soldiers. Many chose to treasure their personal gift from Her Majesty, leaving the contents inside intact. Other soldiers sent them home for safekeeping. A Press Association correspondent reported:

The Queen's chocolate was distributed yesterday amid scenes of great enthusiasm, the troops giving lusty cheers for Her Majesty. The divisional post office presented an animated sight today when the troops, having devoured the chocolate, came to forward the empty boxes to their relatives and friends at home. They are all delighted with the

149. *The Times*, 21 December 1899.

present, and it is almost impossible to obtain a box. As much as £5 [Worth £390 in 2017] was offered for one last night.[150]

It was the intention of many soldiers to send the box home and its contents intact, but the expensive postage charges caused them to eat the chocolate and just send the empty box. Sergeant Cyril Francombe sent his box to his father in Oxfordshire. In a letter dated 29 January 1900, Francombe wrote:

> I am sending the Queen's Chocolate Box home with half its contents … The box, when empty, is neither to be sold nor given away. Officers have offered £1 for them out here, so mind and keep it for me till I get home: it is the message with the Queen's signature that is taking the men's eye, as they feel it is as good as a direct message.[151]

There was such a demand for the Queen's gift that some soldiers chose to sell theirs, with some tins being sold for £20 (£1,500 in 2017). Private Dickenson was among those offered money for his tin. He wrote that 'It was the only present the Queen has ever sent to her soldiers on active service, and you can't get one at any price'.[152]

Private Shepton appealed to his mother, 'Please keep the tin for me, because I value it more than I shall the medal, which I shall get when the war is over, because it is a present from the Queen.'[153]

An anonymous private serving in the Argyll and Sutherland Regiment wrote: 'We have got our chocolates and I have sent my box home as a present to you. I took a small piece out to taste it, but the remainder you can share round the family circle. Remember to look after the box, for it will be an honour to have it years after this.'[154]

Private Humphrey's life was saved as a consequence of Victoria's chocolate box gift at the Battle of Pieters Hill, which was fought between 14 and 28 February 1900. A correspondent reported:

> An army surgeon informs that a case came under his notice in which the Queen's present to her troops saved the owner's life. The box of chocolates was carried in the soldier's haversack. A Mauser bullet struck it, and embedded itself in the chocolate. Otherwise it would have entered the man's spleen. This box is being forwarded to the Queen by Major Daley, the senior medical office at Eastcourt. The man was subsequently wounded in the foot and it was owing to this fact that the case came under my informant's notice. The injured man is Private Humphreys, 2nd Lancashire, a Leigh man.[155]

150. *Bristol Mercury*, 30 January 1900.

151. *Jackson's Oxford Journal*, 3 March 1900.

152. *Burnley Gazette*, 21 February 1900.

153. *Cheltenham Chronicle*, 17 March 1900.

154. *Evening Telegraph*, 27 February 1900.

155. *Leigh Chronicle & Weekly District Advertisers*, 9 March 1900.

91

Royal Herbert Hospital, Woolwich

On 22 March 1900, Victoria visited the Royal Herbert Hospital at Woolwich. Four hundred patients were recovering from their injuries, mainly sustained in Natal. Around one hundred and fifty soldiers had been admitted to the hospital a few days before the Queen's visit, many of whom had been wounded in the relief of Kimberley.

Victoria travelled from Windsor by train directly to Woolwich Arsenal Station to visit the Royal Herbert Hospital. The 2-mile journey from the station to the hospital was lined with approximately 20,000 munition workers from Woolwich Arsenal, who gave her a rapturous welcome. When the Queen arrived at the hospital, she was placed in a wheelchair before being taken to the wards. Bunting had been hoisted everywhere around the hospital.

As the Queen sat beside the bed of each wounded soldier, Lieutenant Colonel Bourke, the principal medical officer, explained their individual cases. In many instances the Queen spoke to the men regarding their wounds and the battles in which they had been engaged, after which she gave them consoling words of comfort. One soldier commented: 'She spoke softly in a low tone, but every word she spoke was quite distinct.'[156] Another soldier remarked: 'She is the kindest lady I ever talked to.'[157] The Queen had brought two large boxes, containing small bouquets of roses, lilies of the valley and other flowers from the royal garden at Windsor, and she presented a small bouquet to each soldier. Several Irish and Canadian soldiers were presented to the Queen during the visit. This was the perfect opportunity for some of the soldiers to personally thank the Queen for her gift of chocolate, which they had received three months' earlier on New Year's Day, but one soldier was so enamoured by his visit from Victoria that he forgot to do this. He recalled:

> I had quite made up my mind to tell her how much we chaps thought of it and how it seemed a sort of reward for everything we'd done, but somehow or other it all seemed to go out of my head. You see it all happened so differently to what I had thought. My notion was that the Queen would just look and there wouldn't be much said, but it wasn't a bit like that. When her Majesty came up I'm blessed if Colonel Bourke didn't tell

---

156. *South London Press*, 31 March 1900.

157. Ibid.

Royal Herbert Hospital is now a residential development known as Royal Herbert Pavilions on Shooters Hill, Woolwich. (Courtesy of David Hallam-Jones; www.geograph.org.uk)

her who I was and how I'd got three fingers off and a bullet in my leg at Spion Kop … He had told the Queen how that I had pretty well pulled round, and the Queen, she said, 'I am very pleased to hear that.' Then her Majesty gave me these beautiful flowers, and I had just time to blurt out, 'Oh, thank you, your Majesty,' when she passed on, and I'd forgotten all about the chocolate.[158]

The Queen also detailed the visit in her journal: 'I was wheeled at once into the wards, first passing through the corridors, lived with Convalescent wounded, but it was so dark I could not see them very well. I was wheeled up to the bed of each man speaking to them & giving them flowers. They seemed so touched & many had tears in their eyes.'[159]

Victoria spent ninety minutes with the wounded soldiers at the hospital, before returning to Windsor Castle during that evening. A correspondent from *The Times* commented that: 'It was a terribly long day's work for a lady of the Queen's age, and she looked somewhat tired.'[160]

---

158. *Penny Illustrated Paper*, 31 March 1900.

159. Royal Archives: RA VIC/MAIN/QVJ (W), 22 March 1900. (Courtesy HM Queen Elizabeth II).

160. *The Times*, 23 March 1900.

Right: Victoria visiting a wounded a soldier at the Royal Herbert Hospital. Appearing in the *Illustrated London News* on 31 March 1900, the sovereign is depicted in a wheelchair, attended by Princess Christian, Princess Victoria of Schleswig-Holstein, Sir Arthur Bigge, private secretary, Lady Antrim, and Emily Lock. (Wellcome Collection)

Below: A view of the Royal Herbert Hospital in Woolwich. Florence Nightingale worked here after returning from the Crimean War, employed by Sidney Herbert, the then Secretary of State for War, to organise the hospital that bears his name. (Wellcome Collection)

92

The Queen's Scarf

This scarf crocheted by Victoria was one of eight awarded to soldiers for 'Distinguished Service' during the South African War.

After visiting wounded soldiers from the South African War at the Royal Herbert Hospital, Victoria sent Field Marshal Lord Roberts (Commander of the British Army in South Africa) eight woollen scarves, knitted by herself, to be given to distinguished soldiers. This scarf was presented to Quartermaster Sergeant H. Clay DCM, 2nd East Surrey Regiment, who was wounded twice during the South African War at Colenso and Vaal Krantz.

Victoria wanted to acknowledge the courage of soldiers who fought in the South African War, not with a medal, but a personal gesture of her gratitude. She made eight scarves using khaki-coloured Berlin wool, personalised with the royal cypher 'VRI' (Victoria Regina Et Imperatrix) crocheted on one of the knots. The scarves were 9in wide, 5ft long, with a 4in fringe at each end.

Lord Roberts confirmed in his dispatch on 1 March 1902 that:

> his Lordship desires to place on record that in April 1900, her late Majesty Queen Victoria was graciously pleased to send him four woollen scarves worked by herself, for distribution to the four most distinguished private soldiers in the Colonial Forces of Canada, Australia, New Zealand and South Africa, then serving under his command. The selection for these gifts of honour was made by the officers commanding the contingents concerned, it being understood that gallant conduct in the field was to be considered the Primary qualification.

Four scarves were awarded to 'the most distinguished private soldier' serving in the British Army, while the remaining four were awarded to colonial soldiers representing Australia, Canada, New Zealand and South Africa.

The four colonial scarves were awarded to Private Richard Rowland Thompson, Royal Canadian Regiment, who rescued wounded comrades at Paardeberg on 18 and 27 February 1900. Trooper Henry Coutts, 1st New Zealand Contingent, was recognised because he rescued

One of eight Queen's Scarves, this example was presented to Colour Sergeant Henry Clay DCM, 2nd East Surrey Regiment. Unfortunately, this scarf was lost during a fire in 2015. However, the museum still holds the scarf presented to Colour Sergeant F. Ferrett DCM, 2nd Queens, Royal West Surrey Regiment. (The Princess of Wales Royal Regiment Museum, Dover Castle)

The Royal Cypher 'VRI' (Victoria Regina Et Imperatrix) embroidered on the scarf presented to Colour Sergeant Henry Clay DCM. (The Princess of Wales Royal Regiment Museum, Dover Castle)

Private Albert du Frayer, of the NSW Mounted Rifles, wearing the Queen's Scarf awarded to him for bravery in South Africa. (Courtesy of the Australian War Memorial; A04542)

a wounded pal who was ambushed at Sanna's Post on 31 March 1900. Trooper Leonard Chadwick was an American citizen who had served with the United States Navy and received the Medal of Honor for valour during the Spanish–American War in 1899. He served with the South African Roberts Horse during the South African War and received the Distinguished Conduct Medal and the Queen's Scarf.

Private Albert Du Frayer, C Squadron, New South Wales Mounted Rifles, was the fourth colonial recipient of the Queen's Scarf. Du Frayer had rescued a dismounted comrade under hostile fire on 11 April 1900. Du Frayer's name contained a list of soldiers recommended for Distinguished Service for this action within New South Wales Military Forces General Order No. 141 on 10 October 1900 and a side note indicated on this list that Du Frayer was 'Awarded Her Majesty's Scarf'.

The four British recipients of the Queen's Scarf were Colour Sergeant Frank Kinsley DCM, serving with the 2nd West Yorkshire Regiment; Colour Sergeant William Colclough, 2nd Devonshire Regiment; Colour Sergeant F. Ferrett DCM, 2nd Queens, Royal West Surrey Regiment; and Colour Sergeant Henry Clay DCM, 2nd East Surrey Regiment.

Victoria intended to personally present the scarves to each of the soldiers, but her death prevented this. George, Duke of York (the future King George V) presented Du Frayer with his in Sydney on 28 May 1901.

The eight scarves were not an official military decoration, however some believed that to have been awarded one was equal to or surpassed the receipt of a Victoria Cross, which was not the case. In 1901, the letters 'Q.S.' denoting 'Queen's Scarf', were listed after Du Frayer's name in the N.W.S. Army and Navy List, which mirrors similarities to how Victoria Cross recipients were listed with the letters 'V.C.' after their names. The person compiling the list may have mistakenly assumed that the award of a Queen's Scarf was a decoration similar to the Victoria Cross, but in the following year the letters were removed and the footnote added to Du Frayer's name with the words 'Awarded the Queen's Scarf for services in South Africa'. In 1938, Du Frayer wrote to Queen Mary, requesting her to ask King George VI to consider granting pensions to recipients of the Queen's Scarf, on a par with Victoria Cross recipients. The War Office replied that a pension for Queen's Scarf recipients did not exist. However, to receive a scarf that was made by Victoria was a great honour.

93

The Last Photograph of Victoria

On 12 December 1900 Victoria visited Windsor Town Hall.

The town hall was hosting an exhibition that promoted trade of Irish products and Victoria expressed an interest to visit privately before the official opening, which was during the afternoon on 12 December.

The Queen had not visited an event of this kind for a number of years and the Irish community appreciated her patronage of Irish manufacturing. Despite living frequently in Windsor Castle during her sixty-three-year reign, it was the first time that she had entered the council chamber in Windsor Town Hall, where there was displayed two full-length portraits of herself and Albert on either side of the royal arms above the mayor's platform.

Victoria's visit was private and once in the council chamber she was introduced to the president of all the Irish industries represented within the exhibition. The Earl of Arran directed the Queen's attention as she spent time at each stall. The *Morning Post* reported that 'before retiring the Queen expressed the pleasure the exhibition had given her, and her appreciation of the efforts to provide employment for those who so greatly need it. Her Majesty made several purchases, and gave special orders to some of the industries.'[161] After spending an hour at the exhibition, she returned to Windsor Castle.

This final photograph of Victoria at the entrance to Windsor Town Hall was taken five weeks before she died. During the weeks that followed she remained active. On 13 December 1900, she held a Privy Council meeting for the Prorogation of Parliament. During that afternoon she met a New Zealand officer who had recovered from wounds sustained in South Africa and who insisted on seeing the Queen before he returned to the war. She also received a Brazilian minister around 5 pm. She wrote in her journal that day that she had lost her appetite.

The following day, 14 December, marked the thirty-ninth anniversary of the death of Albert and she spent some time at his tomb in Royal Mausoleum at Frogmore. She remained feeling unwell. At 5 pm. on 15 December she presented five Victoria Crosses and two Distinguished Service Orders to recipients for bravery during the South African War in her last investiture ceremony at Windsor Castle. The Victoria Cross recipients were Captain Sir John Milbanke

---

161. *Morning Post*, 13 December 1900.

The last photograph of Victoria, which was taken outside Windsor Town Hall on 12 December 1900. (Author's Collection)

VC (10th Hussars), Captain Matthew Meiklejohn VC (2nd Gordon Highlanders), Sergeant H. Eagleheart VC (10th Hussars), Driver Horace Glasock VC (Q Battery, Royal Horse Artillery) and Private Charles Ward (2nd Yorkshire Regiment). They were the last recipients of the Victoria Cross to be decorated by Victoria.

On 17 December she visited the Royal Mausoleum for the final time before going to the Isle of Wight on 18 December to spend Christmas at Osborne House. It was reported that she felt fatigued as a result of the journey. For the past year, the Queen had been suffering from insomnia, lack of appetite and aphasia, affecting her ability to speak. Her physician, Sir James Reid, diagnosed cerebral degeneration. The Prince of Wales was in denial that his mother was seriously ill and returned to London. Reid remained by the Queen's side as current events were hastening her demise. She was anxious about the conflict being fought in South Africa and since 1898 her eldest daughter Vicky had been diagnosed with cancer. On Christmas Eve, Lady Jane Churchill, who served as her lady-in-waiting and companion for fifty years, had died in her sleep at Osborne House, which caused great distress and further exacerbated her melancholic mood. Suffering from rheumatism and failing eyesight, Victoria began the new year downcast, declaring in her journal on 1 January 1901: 'Another year begun, I am feeling so weak and unwell, that I enter upon it sadly.'[162]

Despite her failing health, Victoria received Lord Roberts on 2 January 1901. He had fallen from his horse and had broken his arm, so when he presented himself to the Queen it was in a sling. Victoria had presented Roberts with the Victoria Cross for his conduct during the Indian Mutiny forty-four years earlier. Roberts was able to update her on the progress of the South African War and was able to provide details of the death of her grandson, Prince Christian Victor of Schleswig-Holstein. He was serving as a staff officer for Lord Roberts in South Africa when he died from enteric fever on 29 October 1900. Roberts succeeded in transforming the fortunes of the British Army in the South African War during 1900 and to acknowledge his successes Victoria conferred upon him an Earldom upon and appointed him as a Knight of the Order of the Garter.

On 16 January, Victoria was showing symptoms of mental disorientation. She was confined to a wheelchair and almost blind. Despite her declining eyesight, she continued to write her journal, which she did so from when she was aged thirteen until 13 January 1901, when she wrote her final entry. On 19 January 1901, a Court bulletin was released warning her subjects that the Queen's health had deteriorated. It stated that the 'Queen has not lately been in her usual health, and is unable for the present to take her customary drives.'[163] The Press Association was also authorised to make the following statement on the same date. 'The Queen, during the year, has had a great strain upon her powers which has rather told upon her Majesties nervous system. It has therefore been thought advisable by her Majesties physicians that the Queen should be kept perfectly quiet in the house, and should abstain for the present from transacting business.'[164]

---

162. Royal Archives: RA VIC/MAIN/QVJ (W), 1 January 1901. (Courtesy HM Queen Elizabeth II).

163. *Irish Independent*, 19 January 1901.

164. Ibid.

94

Victoria's Death Bed

In this bedroom in Osborne House, Victoria died at the age of eighty-one from cerebral failure at 6.30 pm on 22 January 1901.

The Queen's health was failing fast and during the evening on 21 January, the royal family assembled around her bedside.

At 8 am on 22 January 1901, the Queen's condition had critically deteriorated to the extent that Dr Reid issued the following bulletin, confirming 'that her Majesty showed signs of diminishing strength, and that her condition was "again" serious.'[165] The royal family assembled at Victoria's bedside, including her grandson, Kaiser Wilhelm II. Dr Reid had secretly informed the Kaiser that his grandmother was seriously ill and the German Emperor insisted on being with her. Given that he had voiced anti-British sentiments, his presence at Osborne House was not welcomed by other members of the royal family.

Victoria was surrounded by her children and grandchildren during her final hours, except for her eldest daughter, Vicky, who was dying from terminal cancer and too ill to make the journey to the Isle of Wight from Germany. Despite showing signs of mental confusion, Victoria was able to recognise the members of her family before she passed away. The Earl of Clarendon and the Lord Chamberlain were also present in the Queen's chamber, as well as the Bishop of Winchester and the Reverend Clement Smith, who read special prayers to the Queen. Kaiser Wilhelm held his grandmother in his arms when she passed away. The Bishop of Winchester conducted a short service in the room in front of the family. Her family and courtiers were unsure about the protocol after Victoria died. Frederick Ponsonby, her assistant private secretary, recalled that 'as the last death of a sovereign had occurred in 1837, no one seemed to know what the procedure was. We spent the evening looking up what had been done when George IV and William IV died.'[166]

Victoria had left explicit detailed instructions regarding her death to Dr Reid three years earlier in December 1897, and he ensured that they were carried out. She ordered that she was not to be embalmed, listed items that she wanted to be placed in her coffin and requested a military state funeral.

---

165. *London Daily News*, 23 January 1901.

166. Ponsonby, op. cit., p.83.

Victoria's bed in Osborne House. (Courtesy of John Simm)

Victoria also stipulated that she did not want to lie in state, and she therefore lay in this bedroom until 25 January. During the morning on 25 January, Professor Herkomer arrived at Osborne House to draw a sketch of the deceased sovereign for Edward VII. In the afternoon, between the hours of 1 pm until 4 pm, servants, members of the royal household, together with petty officers and men serving on the royal yachts were granted the privilege of filing past, entering her room to view her body for one final time. A *Daily News* correspondent spoke to one person who filed past the Queen's body and reported:

The Queen lay on the bed in the room where she died. Over the coverlet were strewn snowdrops and lilies of the valley and a few green sprays, tokens which lay over the body of Prince Albert Victor [Victoria's grandson] at Sandringham. It was not difficult to detect the hand of the Princess of Wales in this arrangement. The hands of the late Queen were folded over the chest and the head leaned somewhat to the right. Over the face had been drawn a white veil of the thinnest texture, through which the features were plainly discernible. Perfect peace was imprinted on the countenance, which, as white marble, like the hands showed no trace of suffering. The illness had left no shrinking, and even the appearance of extreme age had gone.[167]

Another person also recounted the experience of visiting the Queen's bedchamber to view her body:

As I went upstairs, I passed some soldiers … I could not say what regiment they belonged to. It seemed the solemnest moment in my life. I remember feeling nervous and hanging my head, so that I nearly fell, but on such a thick carpet one's boots made no noise. My first feeling was one of surprise. I expected a great and grand gilded chamber, and I thought the bed would be more like a throne. There were a lot of candles all round and someone praying by the bed. It was a very small room, just an ordinary bedroom, only higher. But I really could not tell you much, because I was only there a few minutes, and all the time I was looking at the form of the bed. Yes, while I remember, there was one picture I saw, though there may have been more. It was a picture of Christ hanging on the wall by the bed – that is just over the head. For the dear lady was lying with her head to the wall. How still she was lying. For whenever I see a dead body, that idea always comes over me. After I had crept up to the bed, and was looking on the face, my thought was, how calm and happy she was, like a person in a beautiful sleep. If only she hadn't been so very still! Mind you I had seen her often enough in her little carriage, and once she sent one of her Indian attendants to ask about a little girl that was with me. Once I saw her driving since she came back for the last time; and there she was, hunched up, as you may say, and hanging down her poor head. Well, I said to a neighbour, 'Can that really be the Queen?' It struck me that Lord Roberts must be quick if he wanted the Queen to recognise him. When I saw the sweet face today, it was like what it used to be, and not like then. I hadn't eyes for anything but the face, which had a sort of thin stuff over that you could look through and see it – quite open. What I remember saying to myself is, 'Thank God she died peacefully and without pain.' At the foot of the bed were some wreaths and some flowers. The dear hands were folded across one another, and there was a cross, which I suppose was gold. I remember the rings had to be taken off the figures. Maybe I would have had a lot more to say, only, you see, after the first minute my tears got in the way.[168]

---

167. *Sheffield Daily Telegraph*, 25 January 1901.

168. *Sheffield Daily Telegraph*, 25 January 1901.

95

Poster Proclaiming Victoria's Death

Nations across the British Empire prepared to mourn the death of Victoria.

It was anticipated that large crowds would descend upon London if Victoria was laid in state in the capital, so in order to avoid that scenario, it was decided that her body would remain at Osborne House until 1 February 1901, when her final journey to Windsor via London would begin. Victoria was laid in private in the dining room at Osborne House.

On 24 January 1901, Victoria's body was prepared in accordance with her wishes by Dr Reid and her dresser, Mrs Tuck, who dressed her in a white silk dressing gown, accompanied by garter ribbon and star, and then placed her wedding veil over her face. She had refused to be embalmed, so to alleviate the smell of the corpse, charcoal was scattered at the bottom of her coffin. Victoria's body was then placed in the coffin by her sons and Kaiser Wilhelm II. When they left, Reid and Mrs Tuck carried out Victoria's instructions, which were to be concealed from her children. These secret instructions included the placing of the wedding ring that belonged to John Brown's mother on her finger. A lock of John Brown's hair, his photograph and his pocket handkerchief were placed in the coffin beside Victoria, but concealed from view.

Selected petty officers, serving on the royal yachts, transferred the coffin to the dining room of Osborne House, where it was laid out on a dais a foot above the floor for ten days until her funeral. The coffin was made of fine old English oak and was lined with white satin inside. A silk Royal Standard covered the coffin together with a light drapery of white satin, hung in loops and fastened with white silken tassels. This coffin was later placed in a lead coffin and then another coffin made of old English oak, which would weigh a ton in total.[169]

During the morning on 25 January, a large furniture van arrived at Osborne House containing a supply of palms and other plants for the Queen's lying in state. Also, several bronze candelabras from St Paul's Cathedral arrived to be placed around the coffin. They were conveyed from the wharf at Cowes in vehicles escorted by the coastguard, who assisted in carrying them into the house. These candelabras stood 7ft high and were last used when the Duke of Wellington laid

---

169. *The People*, 27 January 1901.

A poster issued in Toronto carrying the news of Victoria's death and advising of a day of mourning. (Toronto Public Library)

in state in 1852 at the Royal Hospital Chelsea. During the afternoon sixty petty officers and men who served on the royal yachts were allowed the privilege to file past the coffin to pay their last respects to Her Majesty. The Royal Rifle Reserve acted as Guard of Honour on 25 January until the following day, when the Queen's Company of Grenadiers arrived to relieve them. The soldiers stood at attention on the four corners of the coffin, with inverted rifles, with two of her Indian attendants watching over proceedings. On 27 January, journalists were allowed access to Osborne House to file past the Queen's coffin. The coffin was placed upon the Royal Standard with part of the Scottish lion displayed at one corner and the Irish harp at another corner. Extending below that was an Indian shawl. The Queen's Robe of State was draped over the coffin. A journalist reported that 'it was growing yellow with age, that the fur was closer and shorter that the black tips were more numerous and lay more smoothly, than is the case with the ermine of every-day life'.[170]

Victoria's son, Edward VII, placed her Small Diamond Crown upon her coffin. The crown was specifically produced for her return to public life after Albert's death. She refused to wear the Imperial State Crown because it was too heavy and could not be worn over her widow's cap. Victoria commissioned the making of a smaller crown that was lighter, comfortable to wear and could easily be worn above her widow's cap as an alternative. The Small Diamond Crown was made for Victoria during 1870 by crown jewellers R.S. Garrard & Co. The crown formed an openwork silver frame adorned with 1,187 brilliant-cut and rose-cut diamonds in open-backed collet mounts. Victoria continued to dress in mourning for the state opening of Parliament on 8 February 1871 and it was during this occasion that she wore the smaller crown. Victoria wore it on various state occasions and when she received guests at formal gatherings in her palaces. The Imperial Crown was brought to these state occasions, but was rested on a cushion, held close to her.

---

170. *The Times*, 28 January 1901.

96

Isle of Wight Gun Carriage

The actual gun carriage that carried Victoria's body from Osborne House to Cowes.

Given that Victoria was by virtue of her position constitutionally the head of the British Army and daughter of a soldier, it was her wish that her funeral would have a strong military focus and she ordered that her body be transferred on a gun carriage.

At 1.35 pm on 1 February, Victoria's coffin was placed on this carriage by bluejackets from the Royal Navy in the quadrangle of Osborne House, where the King's Company of the Grenadier Guards acted as guard of honour. The Royal Standard was flown at half-mast from the tallest turret of Osborne House. A journalist reported the scene as Victoria embarked on her final journey from the grounds of Osborne House:

> My privileged place was on the lawn immediately facing the Queen's entrance, destined to be the Queen's last exit … The gun carriage and horses of men of 'Y' Battery, Royal Horse Artillery, took up their position on the right hand of the entrance from the point of view of the spectator … And now, at 20 minutes past 1, it became clear that climax was near. A detachment of Hants Yeomanry Carabineers, headed by the three royal grooms in scarlet, went slowly towards the entrance, and in ten minutes there was a stir there also. The Queen's funeral had begun.[171]

The Queen's Highland attendants supported the pall by walking each side of the gun carriage and it was taken to Trinity Wharf, Cowes. On a cushion at the head of the coffin was positioned the great State Crown, alongside a sceptre and two orbs. The royal family walked three abreast behind the gun carriage, headed by King Edward VII, Kaiser Wilhelm II and the Duke of Connaught, followed by the Queen's equerries and servants. They solemnly proceeded to the sound of wailing pipes, muffled drums and the boom of a gun firing a salute from the fleet anchored in Spithead. On exiting the grounds of Osborne House, schoolchildren from the schools in Whippingham, local tenants and local dignitaries lined the street as the cortège passed.

---

171. *The Times*, 2 February 1901.

On arrival at Trinity Wharf, the Queen's coffin was placed aboard the royal yacht *Alberta*. All available warships from the Channel Squadron were ordered to assemble at Spithead on 1 February 1901 so that the transporting of the Queen's coffin across the Solent would make the occasion into an imposing naval display. The British fleet was joined by a squadron of German warships commanded by Prince Henry of Prussia. They formed two lines in the Solent as *Alberta* steamed between these lines of warships, which fired guns while her body was conveyed across.

In the BANQUETING HALL
EDINBURGH CASTLE.
GUN CARRIAGE
which bore the remains of
QUEEN VICTORIA
from Osborne to Cowes, Isle of Wight.

Above: A postcard detailing the gun carriage that transferred Victoria's coffin from Osborne House to Trinity Pier, Cowes. (Author's Collection)

Below: Victoria's coffin leaves Osborne House on 1 February 1901. (Author's Collection)

97

Stereographs of Victoria's Funeral

The death of Victoria was a significant event for the people of Britain and the British Empire, for many had known no other monarch and her passing marked the end of the Victorian era. An outpouring of national grief ensued, which was apparent with the vast numbers of people who lined the streets of London to witness her final journey.

The Queen's coffin remained aboard *Alberta* for the night at Royal Clarence Yard at Gosport, where the Royal Marines Light Infantry provided a vigil. After a short service on 2 February 1901, the coffin was transferred to a train waiting at the private train station in Royal Clarence Yard, which was frequently used by Victoria during her lifetime when travelling between London and Osborne House. The train transported the coffin and the royal family, including Edward VII and Kaiser Wilhelm II, to Victoria station, arriving at 10.51 am. A similar gun carriage awaited her when she arrived at Victoria Station in London, where it began a ninety-minute procession through the streets of London to Paddington Station that passed Buckingham Palace. The bands that escorted the solemn procession played Chopin's *Death March*, amidst the sound of the booming of the minute guns being fired by the Royal Artillery in Hyde Park.

Crowds had assembled along the route of the processions since the early hours of the morning. Many people had travelled by trains from all parts of Britain to pay homage to Victoria. The streets were full of spectators, people were leaning out of windows and many were on roofs clinging to chimney stacks in order to get a good view of the proceedings and a glimpse of the Queen's coffin. All royal palaces and public buildings flew their flags at half-mast in respect of the Queen's passing. There was a huge security operation, the procession from Victoria Station to Paddington Station being lined by 35,000 soldiers and 9,000 policemen.

Four kings and thirty princes were in the procession. Edward VII and Kaiser Wilhelm II rode behind Victoria's coffin. It was believed that Wilhelm II and the Duke of Connaught would ride their horses in line with King Edward's charger, however, the Kaiser, who wore a white uniform and white helmet, was insistent that the British sovereign should be leading the procession behind the gun carriage bearing Victoria's coffin, at all times. 'So punctilious was the German Emperor on this point that when a momentary halt took place on the procession entering Hyde Park, and the King was compelled to pull up his horse, the Emperor William

Above left and above right: Two stereographs showing the gun carriage, coffin and royal mourners as they pass through the streets of London. (Author's Collection)

[sic Wilhelm] immediately checked his steed so that he should not become level with the King, and the Duke of Connaught at once did the same.'[172]

It was reported that 'as the gun carriage with its precious freight came in view everyone seemed to hold their breath. Men could not restrain a sob, and women poured out their grief as if they had lost a near and dear relative.'

At Paddington Station, Victoria's coffin was removed from the gun carriage and transferred upon the royal train, named *Royal Sovereign*, which took her on her final journey to Windsor. There, during that afternoon, a funeral service took place at St George's Chapel, Windsor Castle.

---

172. *Eastern Daily Press*, 4 February 1901.

98

State Funeral Gun Carriage

The State Funeral Gun Carriage that conveyed Victoria's coffin from Windsor Station to St George's Chapel.

Sailors from the Royal Navy came to the rescue when the artillery horses became restive and they had to draw the gun carriage carrying Victoria's coffin through the streets of Windsor. This act would set a precedent where at future state funerals, sailors from the Navy would be granted the privilege of pulling the carriage of the deceased sovereign.

It was a cold day on 2 February 1901 as sailors belonging to the Royal Guard from HMS *Excellent* and guardsmen and horses from the Royal Artillery detailed to draw the gun carriage waited for Victoria's coffin to arrive by train at Windsor. The funeral procession passing through the London streets was behind schedule, which meant that the train carrying the coffin arrived ninety minutes late.

On arrival at Windsor, the coffin was placed on this gun carriage. Cecil B. Levita, one of the Royal Horse Artillery officers on duty that day, wrote that: 'The "gun-carriage" had been specially provided from Woolwich and was fitted with rubber tyres and other gadgets. This was due to Queen Victoria's instructions after seeing a veritable gun-carriage in use at the Duke of Albany's funeral, as also was the prohibition of the use of black horses.'[173]

When the order to move was given, and the drums of the band started to play the *Dead March*, the artillerymen found it difficult to control the horses, because they started to panic and became restless and started to bolt. The Queen's coffin was in danger of falling from the carriage onto the ground, clouding the dignity of the occasion. Cecil B. Levita believed that it was the splinter bar on the carriage that caused the problem, not the horses. He wrote in a letter to *The Times*.

When the royal coffin, weighing about 9cwt, had been placed on the carriage, drums began muffled rolls, which reverberated under the station roof, and the cortège started. Actually, when the horses took the weight, the eyelet hole on the splinter bar, to which the off-wheel trace was hooked, broke. The point of the trace struck the wheeler with

---

173. *The Times*, 28 January 1936.

The State Funeral Gun Carriage that conveyed the coffin from Windsor Station to St George's Chapel on 2 February 1901, being used more than a century later during the ceremonial funeral of Margaret Thatcher on 17 April 2013. (Courtesy of Ronnie MacDonald)

some violence inside the hock, and naturally the horse plunged. A very short time would have been required to improvise an attachment to the gun-carriage.[174]

King Edward VII, Kaiser Wilhelm II, the King of Greece and Prince Louis Battenberg were standing immediately behind and were horrified by the drama that enfolded. Frederick Ponsonby, who was supervising the funeral arrangement, saw Prince Louise Battenberg suggesting in King Edward's ear that the naval guard of honour drag the gun carriage, and the King nodded. Another attempt was made to pull the gun carriage using just two horses, but it was so heavy, it was doubtful that these horses would have been capable of dragging the carriage and coffin up a steep hill in the town. It was suggested to use a short route to transfer the Queen's coffin to St George's Chapel, but it was dismissed because it would have meant disappointing the crowds that had assembled in Windsor who wanted to pay their final respects. Ponsonby then reverted to Prince Louis's suggestion, but the Royal Artillery officers resented the Royal Navy taking charge of the situation. Ponsonby recalled: 'So I determined to adopt Prince Louis's suggestion and accordingly went a second time to the King and said, "Have I your Majesty's permission to take out the horses and let the men of the naval guard of

---

174. Ibid.

Sailors from the Royal Navy pulling Victoria's coffin through the streets of Windsor on 2 February 1901. (Author's Collection)

honour drag the gun-carriage?" The King said, "Certainly." I told the captain of the naval guard of honour to pile arms and bring his men up to the gun carriage.'

The brass plaque attached to the carriage states that it was 'MANNED IN EMERGENCY BY SEAMAN OF THE ROYAL NAVY', during Victoria's funeral. This dramatic and dangerous event would set a precedent because the Royal Navy would be entrusted with the body of the sovereign during funeral processions. This carriage was stored at Whale Island, HMS *Excellent*, in Portsmouth and would be used to carry the body of Edward VII in 1907, George V in 1936, George IV in 1952 as well as Winston Churchill in 1965 and Lord Mountbatten in 1979. It was also used for the ceremonial funeral of Prime Minister Margaret Thatcher in 2013.

99

Victoria's Tomb

Victoria issued precise instructions before her death that her wish was to be buried beside Albert in the Royal Mausoleum at Frogmore.

After the private funeral service that took place at St George's Chapel on 2 February 1901, Victoria's coffin was placed temporarily in the Albert Memorial Chapel within St George's Chapel, where it was watched by the Grenadier Guards.

On 3 February, Albert's tomb was opened and prepared for the Victoria's interment. His sword could be seen lying above his coffin. Modifications had to be made to the tomb, because the Queen's coffin was a third larger than that containing Albert. That meant several inches had to be cut from inside the marble sarcophagus to enable her coffin to be lowered inside.

On 4 February, Victoria's body was transferred to the Royal Mausoleum, Frogmore, by the Royal Horse Artillery.

Edward VII decreed that the public could line the mile and a half route along Long Walk from Windsor Castle to the Royal Mausoleum. At 3 p.m. twelve Grenadier Guards carried Victoria's coffin out of St George's Chapel. Her crown, orb and sceptre, symbols of sovereignty and empire, were surmounted upon her coffin, which was draped with a white silken pall and the Royal Standard. After descending down the steps, the coffin was placed on a khaki-coloured gun carriage, drawn by eight horses from the Royal Horse Artillery. At that precise moment, the bell in the Round Tower of Windsor Castle was tolled. It is only sounded at the death of a sovereign. The procession proceeded through the Norman gatehouse across the Quadrangle, through George IV's archway down the Long Walk, and through the lodge leading from the Long Walk to the Royal Mausoleum, Frogmore. Simultaneously, from the southern end of Long Walk, S Battery, Royal Horse Artillery, the boom of the first of one hundred and one minutes of guns was fired. The Mayor of Windsor ordered that all shops should close during that afternoon. Thousands of people lined the route of Victoria's funeral cortège.

Victoria's body was interred alongside Albert in the marble sarcophagus within the Royal Mausoleum on 4 February.

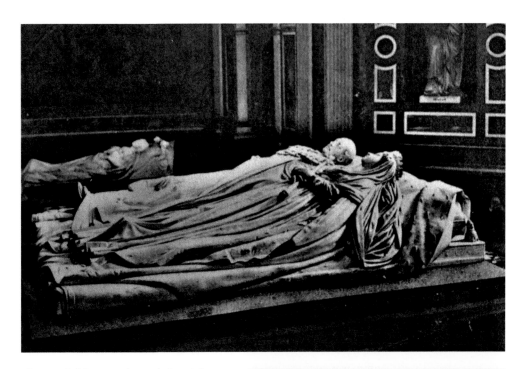

Above and right: Two views of Victoria's tomb in the Royal Mausoleum, Frogmore. (Author's Collection)

100

Queen Victoria Monument at Buckingham Palace

Memorials, monuments and statues were erected all over Britain and its Empire to commemorate the reign. One of those monuments was built outside Buckingham Palace.

Soon after the death of his mother, King Edward VII suggested that a memorial dedicated to Victoria be raised in London. A joint Parliamentary Committee was convened on 19 February 1901 to develop plans and it was decided on 4 March that it should be located in the Mall outside Buckingham Palace. It was estimated that it would cost £250,000 (£19.5 million in 2017) and it was funded by the public, the nation and the British Empire. The money received exceeded the finds required and the surplus was diverted to fund the construction of Admiralty Arch at the eastern end of the Mall.

The Memorial Gardens were designed and created in 1901 by Sir Anton Webb in 1901, comprising flower beds in a semicircular design. The central monument, created by Sir Thomas Brock between 1906 and 1911, was constructed from 2,300 tonnes of white Carrara marble. It stands 25m high and depicts a seated Victoria looking majestically down The Mall towards Admiralty Arch. Statues representing motherhood, truth, victory, charity, constancy and courage, which are associated with Victoria, form part of the design.

The monument was formally opened by Victoria's grandson, King George V, on 16 May 1911, in the presence of Kaiser Wilhelm II of Germany. The King lamented in his speech that the memorial:

> now stands complete before our eyes to revive for us and to convey to our descendants the lustre and fame which shine upon that happy age of British history, when a woman's hand held for a period which almost equalled the allotted span of human life the sceptre of Empire, and when the simple virtues of Queen comforted the hearts of nations ... I pray that this monument may stand for ever in London to proclaim the glories of the reign of Queen Victoria, and to prove to generations the sentiments of affection and reverence which her people felt for her and for her memory ... Her life was devoted to the discharge of her solemn public duty. Her authority was exercised on all occasions with sincere respect for Constitutional usage and tradition. No Sovereign in history reigned so long over so many millions of mankind. No ruler saw so many wonderful changes come

Above: The imposing Queen Victoria Monument that stands in front of Buckingham Palace in London. (Shutterstock)

Right: A sculpture of Victoria, on the monument in front of Buckingham Palace, looking down on the Mall. (Author's Collection)

to pass or witnessed such a vast expansion in the scale and power of human arrangements. No reign in this kingdom ever gathered up more carefully the treasure of the past or prepared more hopefully the path of the future. No woman was ever held in higher honour. No Queen was ever loved so well.[175]

It would take a further thirteen years of work before the memorial was completed in 1924.

---

175. *Pall Mall Gazette*, 16 May 1911.